HAUNTING FLORIDA'S PANHANDLE

Nicole Carlson Easley

Schiffer
Publishing Ltd

4880 Lower Valley Road, Atglen, Pennsylvania 19310

Other Schiffer Books
on Related Subjects:

Florida's Ghosts & Pirates,
978-0-7643-3020-9, $14.99

Greetings from Jacksonville, Florida,
978-0-7643-2958-6, $24.99

Fort Lauderdale Memories,
978-0-7643-2826-8, $24.99

Type set in A Charming Font Expanded/
News Goth BT

ISBN: 978-0-7643-3134-3

Printed in the United States of America

Schiffer Books are available at special discounts for bulk purchases for sales promotions or premiums. Special editions, including personalized covers, corporate imprints, and excerpts can be created in large quantities for special needs. For more information contact the publisher:

Published by Schiffer Publishing Ltd.
4880 Lower Valley Road
Atglen, PA 19310
Phone: (610) 593-1777
Fax: (610) 593-2002
E-mail: Info@schifferbooks.com

For the largest selection of fine reference books on this and related subjects, Please visit our web site at:
www.schifferbooks.com
We are always looking for people to write books on new and related subjects. If you have an idea for a book please contact us at the above address.

This book may be purchased from the publisher. Include $5.00 for shipping. Please try your bookstore first. You may write for a free catalog.

In Europe, Schiffer books are distributed by:
Bushwood Books
6 Marksbury Ave.
Kew Gardens
Surrey TW9 4JF England
Phone: 44 (0) 20 8392-8585
Fax: 44 (0) 20 8392-9876
E-mail: info@bushwoodbooks.co.uk
Website: www.bushwoodbooks.co.uk
Free postage in the U.K., Europe; air mail at cost.

Dedication

To my father, Captain Henry "Skip" Carlson, who once told me, "Don't listen to people who tell you what you can't do; you are the only person who can ever really know what you are capable of," and who can finally stop asking, "When are you going to write a book?"

Acknowledgements

This book would not have been possible without the assistance and support of the following people and organizations:

Jackie Andris, Estella Banta, Susan Bodick, Alyssa Brown, Diane Carlson, Nathan Carlson, Tammy Carlson Beatrice Cotellis, Ashley Chisolm, Betty Davis, Big Bend Ghost Trackers, Wendy Davis, Joel Easley, Jerry Easley, Mary Ellen Easley, Cathy Ebberbach, Scott Ebberbach, Wendy Ebbers, James Elliott, Heather Fuselier, Robert Fuselier, Twana Hall, Mrs. Alfred G. Harms, Louise Heidenreich, Donna Holt, Garnie Holmes, Denise Hill, Pat Inmon, Betsy James, Dianne D. Levi, Auriette Lindsey, Barbee Major, Joan Matey, Bill Mock, Jim Myers, Chandler Myers, Jennifer Myers, Barry Moline, JoAnn Overly, Rai Orszak, Carol Kahn Parker, Captain Jeffrey Pettitt, Lisa Pruitt, Jan Rickey, Reverend Jamie Sanders, Liane Schrader, Sharon Soderholm, Byron Spires, Bill Spohrer, Brenda Thompson, Vicky Tonda, Rodney Walker, Dixie Wright, Harry Wright, Michael Wright, Margaret Zuberbuehler, Amy Zubaly, and Anna Williams

Contents

Introduction

The first real ghost story I remember hearing as a child is one that my father tells. It's still my favorite ghost story because it is nice, even romantic and because it's one of my dad's stories.

When he was a teenager, my father worked as a gravedigger and groundskeeper for the Lands End Cemetery in the small town of Hawleyville, Connecticut. It is one of the oldest cemeteries in the state with graves dating back to the early 1700s. When there was a funeral, he dug the grave by hand with a shovel. He waited in the woods for the funeral to end and the mourners to leave and then filled in the grave.

Mr. Clark was the executer of the cemetery. He and his wife lived just down the hill in a colonial farmhouse. They were well known in the community, especially among the children, because they ran a candy store from the old, one-room Hawleyville Schoolhouse on their property.

The Clarks lost their son to leukemia at a young age. Almost daily, the couple would walk up the hill hand-in-hand to visit his grave. Mr. Clark was a World War I veteran who walked with a limp and used a cane. My father saw them almost every day.

Years later my family was living in New York State. We were on our way to a friend's house in Connecticut. As we were driving down the hilly, windy cemetery road, my parents saw Mr. and Mrs. Clark walking hand-in-hand up the hill toward the cemetery. He was limping along with his cane. She was slouched and scuffling along. They didn't stop to say hello.

That night, my parents mentioned to their friends that the Clarks were still walking up the hill every day to visit their son...just as they had been doing for as long as my father could remember. Their friend replied, "The Clarks have been dead for two years."

Growing up in New England afforded a lot of opportunities for great ghost stories. There was a place not too far from where I grew up called Dudleytown. The original town settlers all died under mysterious circumstances. Legend has it that no bugs or animals exist on the land, no birds fly overhead, and electrical equipment will not function there. Locals discourage talk of Dudleytown. A nearby village even produced a pamphlet that describes the Dudleytown settlement as just another early New England town that didn't survive the harsh winters and illnesses that killed so many settlers in the 1700s. But...they won't tell you where it was located, suspect behavior in an area that celebrates its colonial history with historical markers at every corner. These stories piqued my interest in the paranormal at a young age.

But my first interaction with the supernatural was at my grandmother's house in Brookfield, Connecticut. I was laying awake in one of the twin beds in my grandmother's bedroom. The room was bitterly cold. I felt a paralyzing fear, an odd sensation in a place that was always a haven of comfort for me. It was the kind of fear that makes you acutely aware of your mortality...that heavy, paralyzing, irrational fear that so often grips us in the middle of the night when we are in our beds alone.

Suddenly, the blanket that was folded at the foot of the bed began to move. I watched as the top fold unraveled. It unfolded on me slowly one fold at a time — thump, thump, thump — right up to my chin.

My grandmother said that although she didn't believe in ghosts, late at night, when the house was quiet, she sometimes smelled her mother and felt her touch. I don't remember my great-grandmother, but I did feel a comforting presence in that house. I like to think it was great-grandma Anastasia Bollash Stasny who tucked me in that night.

Later, when I met my husband, Grandma Stasny's presence made itself known. I was in my early 20s and living with my grandmother. I brought Joel home for dinner and to meet grandma.

That night, he had a dream about a woman lying on the floor in the small back bedroom of my grandmother's house. She was holding her neck with both hands. The room was spinning. When he opened his eyes, that same woman was standing in his apartment wearing a long gray dress and a white long-sleeve blouse. She looked surprised to see him.

When Joel told me the story the next day, I smiled. I then told him my great-grandmother died of throat cancer in that little bedroom. Her favorite outfit, the one she wore almost daily, was a long gray dress and long-sleeved white blouse.

What has always interested me about ghosts is that there is so much mystery surrounding what they are and why they are here. In much of the folklore of the dead, they are angry, even evil beings, trying to suck the power out of our camera batteries or seep globs of blood from the walls. I have never had an experience that even remotely fits that description. The stories I hear most often are of family members saying goodbye, like when my aunt listened to a David Bowie marathon on the radio for hours—the favorite music of her recently deceased brother—but when she called the radio station to thank them, they said it never happened.

The Panhandle of Florida is home to some of the most interesting history and folklore of the American South. Small fishing villages dapple the white sandy shores with grand southern homes. Tiny tin-roofed shops that once served as bustling centers of commerce for the cotton trade now offer tourists distraction.

This book is a collection of ghost stories culled from first-hand interviews with those who live and work in haunted homes, theatres, inns, and churches from the Gibson Inn of Apalachicola, to Admiral's Row of the Pensacola NAS.

Before I started researching and writing this book, it had been years since I had experienced anything paranormal. I had begun to suspect that either there was no such thing as ghosts or that I was just no longer sensitive to their presence. I was pleasantly surprised to find that visiting these haunted homes and businesses opened up my senses in a way that I never expected. Not only did I begin to feel energy in some of the locations I visited, but I also started seeing and hearing things in my own home that I cannot explain.

Shortly after visiting the Pensacola NAS, I was standing in my kitchen in front of the dining room window. I saw something large move in the front yard in my peripheral vision. I looked up to see a large, white mass moving quickly across the yard; it looked to be about seven feet tall and seemed to consist of a thick liquid that changed shape as it moved. I ran to the window and looked in the direction it had floated. There was nothing there.

The next day, I heard men's voices in the kitchen so clearly that I turned around expecting to see at least two men standing in our hallway. There was no one there. I checked that the front door was locked, took a deep breath, and decided it must have been my imagination.

That night, I was awakened by something moving slowly in front of my face. I pushed back and said out loud, "Stop it." About an hour later my husband jutted out of bed saying, "Wake up... something's touching my face." Then, our two-year-old started screaming that her nighttime nemesis, Humpty Dumpty, was after her again. We all slept in the bed together that night with the closet light on.

I hope you enjoy reading *Hauntings in Florida's Panhandle* as much as I enjoyed writing it. And maybe, if you're lucky, you'll come away with a little something you weren't expecting as well.

1

Apalachicola

Settlers began arriving in the area that is now the town of Apalachicola in the mid-1820s. It was originally called Cottonton because early settlers believed the land was perfect for growing cotton. By 1831, the town was an important port in the cotton trade and town leaders changed the town's name to Apalachicola to better represent its location on the Apalachicola Bay.

After the Civil War, many Apalachicola residents opted to make a living from the plentiful supply of oysters in the Bay. Apalachicola is now a haven for tourists with a large downtown historic district that features several thoughtfully restored seventeenth century inns and a cemetery where many of the original town settlers enjoy eternal rest.

Gibson Inn

"I was sitting on the lobby couch. I saw a glowing orb float down the staircase. I ran into the bar. It was so cold. It was like being dunked into the beer cooler."

-- Betsy James,
Gibson Inn staff member and tavern musician

Gibson Inn stands out in the small fishing village of Apalachicola as a formidable presence among the gingerbread homes and shops of the historic area just steps away from where the Apalachicola River meets the Gulf of Mexico. Staff believe the Inn is occupied by several "permanent guests."

The Gibson Inn stands out in the small fishing village of Apalachicola. It is a formidable presence among the gingerbread homes and shops of the historic area just steps away from where the Apalachicola River meets the Gulf of Mexico.

The "gray lady" is often seen walking the halls of the second floor of the Gibson Inn of Apalachicola. The apparition has been spotted peeking into guest rooms presumably to make sure the cleaning staff are doing a thorough job. Staff have also seen the apparition of an older woman wearing a house coat on this floor.

On the National Register of Historic Places, the Gibson Inn is a trip back in time. Its thirty guest rooms feature period antiques and much of the Inn has its original woodwork and floors. Almost every meandering hall leads guests to the grand white porch that wraps around the Inn as if to hold tight its vintage charm. It offers guests wooden rocking chairs and a view of the bay and downtown. But, according to staff and many guests, views and quaint shops are not the only thing visitors are likely to encounter during a stay at the Gibson Inn.

Built in 1907 by James Fulton Buck, the Inn was originally known as the Franklin Hotel. James was a wealthy and well-established businessman in the lumber industry. The Franklin Hotel was the only first-class hotel between Pensacola and Jacksonville that was heated entirely by steam.[1]

In 1917, sisters Annie and Mary Ella Gibson were charged with the management of the property. They purchased the Inn in 1923 and renamed it the Gibson Inn. In 1942, the United States Army commandeered the property for use as an officers' club and billets hall.[1]

After the war, the Gibson Inn changed ownership many times. It served the area as a boarding house and saloon. In the 1970s, the first floor was divided into retail space. The Inn slowly slipped into disrepair. In 1985, Neil and Michael Koun and Michael Merlo purchased and restored the property.[1]

According to staff, there are at least nine documented "permanent guests,"

Guests of the Gibson Inn have seen the apparition of a young girl weeping on a ledge from the third floor hall and on the stairs leading to room 315.

as housekeeping staff affectionately refer to them, residing in the guest rooms and halls of the Gibson Inn. Some are seen only in specific areas of the Inn—staff keeps an eye out for them in specific hallways and guest rooms. Others seem to travel at will and are reported by guests and staff at different times of the day in various areas of the Inn.

The staff also say that some of their permanent guests keep an eye out for present-day guests, even getting "playful" and interacting with them by re-arranging their belongings, moving furniture, and, at times, gently pinching female guests' bottoms. The staff believe that among their permanent guests are two sea captains they refer to as Captain Duncan and Captain Woods.

Margaret Zuberbuehler is the Inn's head housekeeper and a second generation "sensitive." *A sensitive is a person who is sensitive to energy within and beyond the physical world.* Margaret, who often sees the Inn's permanent residents, describes Captain Duncan as a man in his late 30s or 40s. He is about 5'7 and slim. He wears a work shirt, tan pants, and white rubber boots—a description that has been confirmed by Captain Duncan's ancestors.

Margaret describes Captain Woods as a plump man. He wears a dark blue jacket and tan pants. Staff believe that both Captain Duncan and Captain Woods, a former officer in the Army Corp. of Engineers, became ill from pneumonia while at sea, took refuge in the Inn, and died from their illnesses in guest rooms 315 and 309 respectively. According to Innkeeper Susan Bodeck, room 309 is considered the most haunted guest room in the Inn.

"309 is the guest room we call the Captain's Room," says Susan. "That's the room guests stay in if they have an interest in having an experience with one of our permanent guests."

Although the staff don't completely agree on who is haunting room 309, they do agree that it's a male and that he enjoys the company of female guests. Female guests staying in the room regularly comment that they were pinched on the bottom while laying in the bed or walking around the room in the evening. They have also reported being gently touched by unseen hands that "tucked" them into bed at night.

One couple staying in the room was awakened separately during the night. The woman woke up sensing that there was something in the room looking at her. She lay there in the darkness for a moment waiting for her eyes to adjust. Suddenly, she felt the mattress push down behind her as if someone had leaned on it. She glanced at her husband, who was sound asleep, and continued to lay still as she felt large fingers push the bed blankets under her back and bottom and then...a light pinch on her bottom.

She heard something move from the side of the bed across the hardwood floor mumbling in a deep voice, and then saw a black shadow walk in front of the alarm clock blocking its light. She blinked and it was gone.

Later that night, the man was awakened by something very close to his face pushing on his shoulder and moaning in his ear.

"It was a strange sensation," says Alyssa, a Gibson Inn guest. "It wasn't really scary. It seemed almost caring. His voice sounded thoughtful, almost worried."

Friendly pinching is not the only thing the spirit of room 309 is known for. Another couple staying in the room had a similar experience of being cared for. The woman awakened in the middle of the night feeling very cold. She woke her husband and asked him to get her a blanket from the closet. He refused and she fell back asleep. In the morning, the couple woke to find a blanket from the closet was tucked neatly around both of them.

"Captain Duncan likes things to be to be calm and quiet," says Margaret. "Most guests find a lot of peace in that room. We have had couples on the verge of breaking up stay in that room and find so much contentment there, that they stay together and come back to stay in that room again and again."

But, Margaret says, "You shouldn't get into an argument in guest room 309."

One couple staying in 309 did get into an argument. The very passionate couple had been having a heated argument in the room. After yelling at each other for several hours, they grew tired and went to sleep. Captain Duncan apparently sided with the man.

During the night, the woman was suddenly and forcefully pushed out of the bed and onto the floor. Assuming it was her husband, she got up on her knees and reached for the lamp on the side table to protect herself. When she arched back to threaten him, there was no one in the bed. The man had been in the bathroom for some time.

Many guests of room 309 in the Gibson Inn have been playfully pinched on their backside and "tucked" into bed at night. Inn staff believe the room is still home to a sea captain who died of pneumonia.

A female guest who was traveling alone also had an interesting interaction with the Captain. She had settled into the room and unpacked her belongings. She laid all of her clothes out on the bed and went downstairs for dinner. When she returned to her room that evening, she found that all of her clothes had been placed neatly back in her suitcase.

Staff say there are a lot of complaints to housekeeping about items having been moved from the bed of guest room 309—many times when the room has not yet been serviced. Many guests who leave the bed unmade and go downstairs for breakfast find that the bedcovers have been thrown around the bed or that the bed has been haphazardly made. Items left on the bed are often moved and placed around the room.

The television in the room changes channels seemingly by itself. One member of the housekeeping staff who enjoys watching soap operas while she services the rooms does not watch them in guest room 309. Because, she says, every time she turns on the television to watch a soap opera, the channel changes by itself.

Guest room 309 is not the only room where staff and guests have had experiences with the Gibson Inn's permanent guests.

The tavern of the Gibson Inn as it looked in 1907 and as it looks today. Both a guest and staff member have had the odd experience of walking into the tavern and seeing it, and its patrons as if it were the 1940s, a time when the tavern area of the Inn had been commandeered by the United States Army as an officers' club.

Staff regularly hear heavy breathing coming from guest room 315. Although no one has ever reported a negative experience in the room, several members of the housekeeping staff will not go into the guest room alone.

The lights in guest room 315 often turn off at midnight and, for no technically known reason, will not turn back on. Housekeeping staff say that it is a difficult room to service because fresh towels placed on racks and folded on shelves are found on the floor moments later. Cleaning products left out are moved to other areas of the room.

One member of the housekeeping staff reported a very unsettling experience while servicing guest room 315. After making both of the room's twin beds and tidying the room, she decided to take a short break and get some fresh air. She placed several bottles of cleaning products on top of one of the beds and stepped out to the porch for few moments. When she returned to the guest room several moments later, the bottles of cleaning products she had placed on the bed were on the floor. Both of the beds in the room had been disheveled and several items of furniture in the guest room had been re-arranged.

Those staying in guest room 315 have also experienced the furniture in the room being re-arranged. Two guests staying in the room woke on the second day of their stay to find that the two chairs that had been facing the center of the room were facing the window...as if someone had been sitting enjoying the view.

A pair of men's shoes that had been left with the laces untied by the side of the bed were found in the same spot...but with the laces tied. A pen and pad that had been left at the foot of the bed were placed neatly on the nightstand. The guests moved the chairs back where they had been and left the room as it was. That evening they went to dinner leaving their beds unmade. When they returned, the sheets and covers on both of the beds had been untucked and thrown about the beds as if they had been haphazardly made.

Inn guests staying on the third floor often complain that there is a cold spot in the hallway near guest room 315. One guest even believes she may have caught a glimpse of the source of the cold spot. The guest was walking on the second floor toward the stairway that leads to the third floor. She looked up and saw what appeared to be a young girl, possibly a teenager, standing on the porch sobbing into her hands. A heavy mist surrounded her, but the woman could see that she had brown hair set in ringlets and she was wearing a long dress.

Most sightings of the Inn's permanent guests occur on the second floor, and many guests have encountered the apparition that staff refer to as the "gray lady." Inn housekeepers are very familiar with the apparition, who tends to make herself known if anyone leaves trash or linens in the hallway, which is something that's not allowed at the Inn.

Unwitting guests have seen the gray lady as well. One guest, who was visiting the Gibson Inn from Canada, spotted the gray lady walking purposefully down the hallway. She was wearing a long gray dress with a white apron. Her gray hair was tied neatly in a bun on the top of her head. The guest asked at the desk what position the woman served with the Inn, commenting that she seemed "out of place."

Another guest encountered the gray lady in the hallway. He walked up to her to ask her a question. The lady quickly turned her head and walked away from him, disappearing down the hallway. Other guests of the Inn have experienced the same interaction with the gray lady. Many guests have stopped in the hallway to smile at her or say, "hello." Her response is always to look away and walk quickly down any available hallway.

"One guest pulled me aside and asked me if we had 'spooks,'" says Margaret. "Occasionally, guests will complain that a member of housekeeping would not answer their request for more towels or answer a question. I have to explain to them that the lady in the long, gray uniform dress hasn't worked here for some time.

"But most guests who encounter the gray lady can tell right away that she is one of our permanent guests."

In addition to sightings of the gray lady, staff say that guests staying in rooms 207 and 210 often comment that they feel as though they are being watched. Housekeeping staff members say that servicing guest room 207 is similar to servicing guest room 315—fresh towels hung or folded and placed on shelves in the bathroom are found on the floor just moments later.

Several guests staying on the second floor have complained to staff that a "dirty" workman on their floor is making them uneasy. A young woman staying in guest room 213 called downstairs to complain that a "very dirty man with a tool box" was standing outside her door.

"We do have workmen occasionally at the Gibson," says Margaret. "But we don't employ anyone who fits the description of 'dirty' and we didn't have any workmen in the Inn that day."

Also on the second floor, Margaret spotted a young woman wearing a white shirt and brown pants walk into guest room 210. She followed the woman because she knew that room was unoccupied. When she walked into the room, though, the woman was gone.

Local historians believe that in the 1970s several rooms on the second floor of the Gibson Inn served the town as a house of ill repute. Staff say that second-floor guests sometimes complain that there is a party in the room next to theirs. Staff has heard complaints of laughing, giggling, drinking, and boisterous conversation coming from empty rooms.

"We take complaints of noise very seriously," says Susan. "Unfortunately on the second floor, it can be difficult to locate the partiers."

The permanent guests of the Gibson Inn also make themselves known on the first floor. Guests staying in room 101 often comment that they feel someone is "watching" them. One guest commented to staff several times that she felt there was someone in the room with her. Margaret, who happened to be working with the staff to service the rooms on the first floor that day, believes she saw what was bothering the guest. While servicing room 101, Margaret felt someone looking at her. She looked toward the guest room door and saw an older woman wearing a housecoat standing in the hallway and peeking into the room. Margaret greeted the woman with a 'hello' and asked her who she was. The woman in the housecoat looked at her without expression and then faded away.

The Inn's tavern, just outside of the lobby, is a popular place for guests and town residents to gather. It is also a popular area for the Inn's permanent guests to have a little mischievous fun with both staff and guests.

Late one evening, Susan and staff member Betsy James were carrying a case of beer from the kitchen to the bar. The kitchen was dark. Suddenly they both felt a gush of air pass by their faces as if something had been thrown between them as they were walking. Then they heard a clunk as if something small and heavy had hit the floor. When they turned on the light, a salt shaker from the kitchen was rolling around on the tavern floor.

On another evening, Betsy was sitting on the couch in the lobby that sits across from the staircase to the second floor. She looked up and saw a glowing orb about three inches wide float down the stairs. A bit spooked, she got up and ran into the bar, which had become frigidly cold.

"It became so cold so quickly," said Betsy. "It was like being plunged into the beer cooler."

On another occasion, Betsy and an Inn guest watched in awe as a wine glass that was sitting on the bar began to move back and forth by itself. The glass tipped slowly and with a controlled motion from side to side several times. It then lifted about an inch and a half into the air. It hovered for a moment, and then flew into a nearby garbage can.

One evening, a staff member decided to change a light bulb over the bar that had blown out days earlier. She pulled a chair behind the bar and climbed up on it to reach the blown bulb. Just as her fingers were about to touch the bulb, it lit up. The bulb burned for several more days.

The Gibson Inn is not just home to human permanent guests. Over the years, guests have seen the Inn's former house cats napping on the furniture in the lobby, walking sheepishly, and running through the halls. Housekeeping staff have also reported seeing a small shaggy dog running around on the second floor. He seems to always be one step ahead of anyone trying to catch him.

"One of our guests approached me very angrily," said Susan. "He said he was told he could not have pets in the Inn, but that there clearly were cats sleeping in the lobby.

"He described each of the cats to me in great detail — a black and white cat laying on the desk, a striped cat laying on the couch, and another striped cat running down the hallway and vanishing.

"He was pretty surprised when I told him, 'Yes, those were our house cats, but they died years ago.'"

Although it is a common occurrence for staff and guests to see the Inn's permanent guests in the present, on at least a couple of occasions they have seen these residents in their own time.

"Sometimes we go into a time warp," says Margaret.

On several occasions, Margaret has walked down the lobby stairs toward the tavern and noticed immediately that it looks different. The decorative wall between the Inn lobby and the tavern is gone. The tavern bar is pushed farther toward the back wall. Men in World War II uniforms are standing and sitting in the tavern drinking and talking.

"If they look at you," she says, "they fade away and the room returns to present day."

At least one guest at the Inn had a similar experience in the tavern. He was sitting at the bar drinking a beer. He thought he was alone in the tavern, but heard several male voices behind him. He turned to look behind him—and noticed that the room looked very different.

Two long rectangular tables had replaced the small round tables that were in the tavern when he sat down. Four men were sitting at one of the tables. He turned back to the bar. It was at least a foot farther away from him than it had been. He sat there for a moment holding his beer in his lap. The voices stopped. He turned cautiously toward the men. They were gone. In their place were empty round tables. The tavern looked as it did when he walked in.

"That man never did come back," says Margaret. "But that's rare for the Gibson. There is something about this place. People come here and they don't want to leave."

(Author's note: Some of the names in this story were changed to protect the identy of contributors.)

Coombs Inn

"There was a shadowy figure of a man in a dark suit with a pocket watch reflected in the glass of the dining room door. He was watching us. He walked through the side of the house and then through the wall."

-- Estella Banta,
Coombs Inn manager

The Coombs Inn of Apalachicola was built in 1905 by James and Maria Coombs. It was their dream home until a devastating fire in 1911 greatly damaged their home and their will to live. It has been restored to a light and bright town fixture sitting across from the city's historic Chestnut Cemetery.

The Coombs Inn of Apalachicola is a light and bright town fixture sitting across from the city's historic Chestnut Cemetery. The cemetery serves as the final resting spot for almost all of the original town settlers, many Yellow Fever

The Coombs Inn had fallen into serious disrepair in 1978 when Bill Shoher and Lynn Wilson purchased the property.

Members of the housekeeping and management staff of the Coombs Inn often hear children's laughter emanating from guest rooms on the second floor where it's likely the Coombs' children spent much of their childhood.

victims, Civil War soldiers, and some who thought they were just passing through. The graves of James and Maria Coombs and a few members of their extended family are just a short walk from their beloved home.

James and Maria were childhood sweethearts growing up in Old Town, Maine. James served in the Civil War for a nine-month tour of duty with the 28th Maine Voluntary Infantry Regiment under General Sherman. He was stationed in Donaldsville, Louisiana. After several skirmishes, the regiment was moved to New Orleans where they boarded a ship and traveled back to Maine. James married Maria and in 1871 the couple relocated to Pensacola where James worked in the burgeoning timber industry. The couple experienced great success and soon purchased the Franklin County Lumber Company.[2]

It is rumored that Theodore Roosevelt asked James to run as his vice president in the 1904 Presidential election. If the rumor is true, James turned Roosevelt down. It was around this time when James decided that his family needed a home that better represented their financial success and social standing.[2]

The Coombs settled in Apalachicola and began building their dream home. James and Maria took great care choosing all of the objects and elements of their home. They incorporated every

The apparition of a man in a dark suit with a pocket watch has been seen walking from the dining room of the Coombs Inn to a first-floor guest room that once served as the Coombs' music room. The same apparition has been seen reflected in the glass of the dining room door.

luxury item money could buy. The home was a showcase for its time with nine coal-burning fireplaces. Decorative wood lined the home's walls and ceilings. Maria was especially proud of the home's furniture and linens that had been shipped from Europe.[2]

The Coombs lived happily in the home for several years. Then, at midnight on March 6, 1911, a fire sparked in the attic. The Coombs were able to escape the blaze that engulfed their home, but by the time the area's three volunteer horse-drawn fire companies put out the flames, the house had been badly damaged and all of their possessions destroyed.[2]

The Coombs family spent that night in the Franklin Hotel (now the Gibson Inn). James planned for the family to stay at the Inn

Female guests staying in the former bedroom of James and Maria Coombs at the Coombs Inn often are awakened by an unseen hand gently brushing their cheek.

until they could rebuild their home. Maria fell into a deep depression and died in her bed ten days after arriving at the Franklin Inn. James was devastated by his loss. He died three weeks later of an unknown cause. In the years that followed, the Coombs' home was repaired and several generations of Coombs lived there. By the 1960s, the upkeep on the large home had become too much for the Coombs' decedents to manage. The home was abandoned and fell into serious disrepair.[2]

In 1978, Bill Spoher and Lynn Wilson noticed the dilapidated home while vacationing in Apalachicola. The couple was intrigued by the home and began the several-year search to find its owners and purchase the property. In 1994, after a renovation project, James and Maria's home and property were restored to their former elegance. The Coombs Inn has since welcomed area tourists to relax in its rooms, enjoy Apalachicola's history and small-town flair, and perhaps have a brush with the past.

Coombs Inn staff have seen the apparitions of children playing in the upstairs guest rooms and heard their laughter waft down the large wooden staircase to the Inn's parlor. Inn manager and resident, Estella Banta, hears the laughter and playful noises regularly from her desk in the lobby. Staff believe the Coombs'

James Coombs poses with stuffed alligators. Coombs Inn staff and guests have seen the apparition of a man wearing a dark suit walking through walls and reflected in the glass of a dining room door.

children spent much of their time in two of the guest rooms on the second floor. Housekeepers have seen children playing in their peripheral vision while servicing guest rooms five and six on the second floor. They often hear children's laughter emanating from those guest rooms.

In addition to the presence of ghostly children, the Coombs Inn may also harbor the spirit of a flirtatious gentleman. Guests staying in the former bedroom of James and Maria on the second floor often are awakened by unseen fingers gently brushing the side of their face.

"Several women who have stayed in that guest room have said the same thing," says Bill Spoher, Coombs Inn owner. "They comment that they enjoyed their stay, but that they were awakened nightly by someone caressing their cheek."

Staff and guests believe they may have seen the flirtatious gentleman walking from the dining room on the first floor into one of the first-floor guest rooms and on another occasion, reflected in the glass of the dining room door.

In September of 2004, staff were preparing for the arrival of Hurricane Jeanne. Estella and another staff member were boarding up windows outside of the dining room—and both of them saw the reflection of a man wearing a dark-colored suit in one of the dining room windows.

"It was a shadowy figure," says Estella. "He was looking toward us as if he wanted to communicate something, perhaps to thank us for protecting his home. We felt compelled to look."

On another occasion, staff members saw what appeared to be the same man standing outside of the same dining room window. Two staff members watched as the man walked through the wall where there once had been a door and then...disappear.

A new staff member, who had not heard the stories of the Coombs Inn, followed a man fitting the same description as he walked from the dining room through the parlor and into one of the first-floor guest rooms that once served as the Coombs' music room. She was flustered when she walked into the guest room and the man was not there.

The gentleman in the dark suit is not the only adult apparition that has been seen walking about the Coombs Inn. A guest staying at the Inn was startled when he saw a woman wearing a long, heavy dress brush by him in the parlor. When he turned to greet her, he found that he was alone.

On several different occasions staff have seen a handyman they did not recognize working on the hinges of one of the first-floor guest rooms. When staff approach the man, he moves away from them and disappears into the room. Staff often find the hinges unscrewed on the door.

"I'm not a superstitious person," says Bill, "but who or whatever is here seems happy and at peace with itself and what we have done with the home."

Private Residence

I was on the front porch delivering the mail. I heard someone open the screen door and walk outside. I turned around and looked into the house. There was no one there.

-- James,
former Apalachicola mail carrier

There is a mansion in Apalachicola that locals quietly call the "demon house." Real estate agents have refused to show the home after their first visit. Those who spend the night are never quite the same.

The home was owned for years by Alfred D., who grew up there with his family. They were devoutly religious and did not believe in ghosts. They regularly saw and heard the apparitions of a man and a child walking up the main staircase in the front of the home. Doors opened and closed by themselves and toys were played with by unseen hands. They called their home's permanent residents... *its demons*.

The owner of the property does not like to talk about the home's "demons." Townspeople who try to discuss the home's odd reputation are usually answered with, "Shhh, don't talk about them."

Those who have spent any time in the home know that the apparition of a man in a suit walks around the downstairs. And sometimes at night there is a rumbling and a gust of wind as if a freight train is traveling through the home.

On one occasion, a friend was staying in the home sleeping in the living room. He was awakened by the sound of heavy footsteps walking down the stairs. He sat up and looked toward the stairs. He saw a red ball bounce to the floor. Thinking that he must have heard the ball bouncing down the stairs, he walked up to it. When he got within a foot of the ball, it flew across the room in the opposite direction as if it had been kicked.

A realtor who visited the empty property entered through the front door and heard so much movement on the wooden floors and stairs that she ran out the front door and vowed never to return.

James, who was a young mail carrier when he visited the home, was in the habit of walking the mail up to the front porch and handing it to Alfred. One day, he walked onto the porch and knocked, but no one answered. He turned around to leave, but then heard the door squeak open and footsteps stepping out onto the wooden porch. He turned with the mail in his hand, but there was no one there.

"I had heard Alfred make comments about what he called demons," says James, "but until you experience something for yourself, you just don't understand."

(Author's note: Some of the names in this story were changed to protect the identy of contributors.)

2

Pensacola Naval Air Station

The site of the Pensacola Naval Air Station was settled by the Spanish in the 1500s. In 1698, the Spanish built Fort San Carlos de Austria on the land to defend their newly established port. In 1719, amid much squabbling over land rights, French forces destroyed the Fort. In 1763, Britain gained control over the sought-after land and built a protective wooden structure, the Royal Navy Redoubt.

In 1787, Spain once again contolled the land, building a sea-level artillery battery, Bateria de San Antonio, and protective fort, Fort San Carlos de Barrancas.

By 1821, the area and the Fort belonged to the United States. The wooden fort was replaced by a brick structure and became known as Fort Barrancas. In 1826, the U.S. began building a naval yard at the site. The towns of Warrington and Woolsey sprung up to house craftsmen and other workers.

Many buildings on the Fort were destroyed and rebuilt following the Civil War and the devastation of several hurricanes. In 1911, the first aircraft carrier was built. By World War I the Pensacola Naval Air Station had thirty-eight naval aviators and fifty-four airplanes.[3]

Pensacola Lighthouse

"I was closing up by myself. I went to close the cellar door. I looked down. The lights were all out. As I closed the door, I heard footsteps. It sounded like someone was walking up the cellar stairs, out of the door and down the hallway toward the front door. And when it got to there, why, it went right through it."
-- Dianne Levi,
Pensacola Lighthouse Volunteer

The Pensacola Lighthouse has been keeping watch over the Pensacola Bay and its many sea captains since 1859. It has stood steadfast through hurricanes, lightning strikes, and Civil War fire. It stands as a symbol of Pensacola's calm resilience to war, violent storms, and the unforgiving evolution of time. It seems alive in its unwavering solicitude to the sea and its travelers, an attribute that has been shared by many of its keepers whose families lived and died within its protective walls.

The original Pensacola Lighthouse was built in 1824. It did not stand at its post for long—the tower was too short. Ship captains couldn't see the light and the mechanism to turn the clock that ran the light often broke. Jeremiah Ingraham was the Lighthouse keeper until his death in 1840. Jeremiah's wife Michaela took over his duties as Lighthouse keeper until 1855. With her death, Joseph Palmes, the Ingrahams' son-in-law, became the Lighthouse keeper.[4]

Joseph continued to serve as keeper in 1858 after the new Pensacola Lighthouse was constructed. The new Lighthouse stood alone on the stark beach. A heavy solid mahogany door at the base of the tower was the only entrance. The only quarters for the keepers was a small room over the oil storage room at the base of the tower. Later a duplex home was built at the base of the

The Pensacola Lighthouse on the Naval Air Station (NAS) has been keeping watch over the Pensacola Bay and its many sea captains since 1859. It has stood steadfast through hurricanes, lightning strikes, and Civil War fire. NAS staff have seen and heard apparitions of Lighthouse keepers from the past still making their rounds.

Several volunteers of the Pensacola Lighthouse have heard footsteps and movement as if someone unseen were walking casually up the basement steps and down the hallway.

tower to provide housing for a lead keeper and an assistant.[4]

Over the years, many men and women staffed the tower that kept watch over the Pensacola Bay, but the keeper who staffed the Lighthouse for the longest was George Tucker Clifford. George was assigned to serve as assistant Lighthouse keeper on September 18, 1885.[4]

In 1886, George became lead keeper, a position he retained for thirty-one years. His daughter, Ella, who was four when the family moved into the Lighthouse, grew up there and was married in the Lighthouse in 1903. In November of 1904, Ella gave birth to a baby girl named Naomi. Five months later, Ella died in the Lighthouse of an unknown cause.[4]

Today the Lighthouse duplex or keepers' quarters houses a museum on the first floor and military offices on the second floor. There is a quiet understanding between museum staff and military personnel that they are not alone in their appreciation of the Lighthouse...nor are they the only ones going about their daily business within its walls.

It is common for Lighthouse doors, including the front door to the keepers' quarters and the original solid wood Lighthouse tower door, to open and slam shut seemingly by themselves—as

Volunteers and guests of the Pensacola Lighthouse have witnessed the solid wood door that has guarded the entrance to the Lighthouse tower for more than one hundred years slam shut forcefully by unseen hands.

does the fifty-pound iron hatch at the top of the Lighthouse tower.

In addition to slamming doors, the unexplained sounds of footsteps resonate from the tower stairs and the original wood flooring of the keepers' quarters. The smell of a tobacco pipe lingers in the air even though smoking has long been prohibited in the keepers' quarters and in the Lighthouse tower. Disembodied screams and male voices cursing emanate from the

During the 1994 renovation of the Pensacola Lighthouse, maintenance workers found a rope they had been unable to dislodge from water pipes in the basement, hanging in the shape of a noose in the command room of the Lighthouse.

Local school children and volunteers have witnessed the door in the command center of the Pensacola Lighthouse slamming shut by an unseen force. Visitors to the Lighthouse have also reported having their camera pulled by the strap from their shoulder in this room.

Lighthouse tower. Objects in the keepers' quarters are thrown or moved from room to room and temperatures in the keepers' quarters and in the tower fluctuate wildly regardless of the temperature outside.

Reports of strange happenings in the Lighthouse date back to the 1930s when the duplex still served as the keepers' quarters. Writings from that time record residents hearing the ever-present sounds of footsteps on the wooden floor leading from the tower to the front door of the keepers' quarters, disembodied voices in the keepers' quarters, and heavy breathing in the tower.

Dianne Levi, an area historian and a board member of the Florida Lighthouse Association, has collected stories over the years documenting some of the strange happenings in the Pensacola Lighthouse.

Emmitt Hatten lived in the keepers' quarters of the Lighthouse while his father served as keeper from 1931 to 1953. Emmitt was often charged with small chores to help his father and mother in their daily duties including climbing the Lighthouse tower to pull the chains that kept the Lighthouse lens turning.

Emmitt often heard heavy breathing in the Lighthouse when he knew he was alone. He and his mother also heard loud creaking on the stairs of the keepers' quarters nightly. Emmitt's mother would send him downstairs to see who was walking around in their home. On one occasion, Emmitt ran to the stairs and called out, "Who is here?" The sound of footsteps on the stairs stopped. He heard the front door to the keepers' quarters open and then shut. Emmitt ran up the stairs to the second story and peered out of the window at the front gate. He watched as the Lighthouse gate opened and shut as if an invisible person had walked off the porch and through the front gate.

In September of 1974, the widow of Navy Lieutenant Commander Ann St. John rented the Lighthouse for a week's stay. She was preparing to attend a party on a quiet, warm day. She was on the second floor of the keepers' quarters when she heard a series of rapid knocks on the outside of the window as if someone was trying to get her attention.[5]

She walked out onto the second-floor porch. There was no one on the porch and she found that there was no access to the porch from the ground. Ann went back inside the quarters and continued to get ready. Within minutes, the knocking began again. She packed her things and left the Lighthouse.

On a rainy evening in 1977, Coast Guardsman Rick Lumpkin was walking down the Lighthouse tower steps from the lantern porthole. He was about fifteen stories high when he heard a rustling sound against one of the Lighthouse windows. Rick edged off of the staircase and slid onto the brick ledge at the edge of the wall. He peeked through the Lighthouse window. He stared in awe at the apparition of an elderly woman sitting in a rocking chair floating. She smiled at him. He blinked and she was gone.[5]

In November of 1977, Leroy Page was in the Lighthouse with a lady friend. She accompanied him as he completed the evening's final check of the machinery. As they were walking down the tower stairs, they both heard a soft female-sounding laugh. Puzzled, they turned around and began the climb back to the top of the tower. They reached the top and opened the hatch, but could not find the source of the laughter. As they were walking back down the tower steps, the laughter began again and emanated through the tower until they reached the bottom steps.[5]

One of the strangest and most ominous occurrences in the Lighthouse happened during the 1994 renovations of the keepers' quarters. A maintenance crew was working in the basement beneath the keepers' quarters and the command room that connects the keepers' quarters to the Lighthouse tower. They were attempting to dislodge an old rope that was tightly wound around several water pipes. After working for more than an hour, they decided to take a break on the first-floor front porch of the keepers' quarters.

After about twenty minutes, the crew headed back inside the keepers' quarters. As they were walking toward the command room and the basement stairs, they noticed that a rope was hanging from the ceiling in the command room. As they got closer, they realized it was the rope from the basement. It had been detangled and was now hanging in the command room from a ceiling fixture in the shape of a noose.

Although this is one of the most well-told stories of maintenance workers feeling as though something in the Lighthouse was trying to get their attention during the renovation, it is only one of many. Renovation workers were plagued with disruptions and disturbances; their electrical cords were restricted by unseen obstacles and often yanked out of their hands by unseen forces, and extreme temperature fluctuations left them shivering with cold on hot summer nights.

On one occasion, men working on the grounds just outside of the control room watched in awe as a long-ago disconnected water pipe suddenly pushed out of the ground and shook violently as if water was forcefully gushing through it.

That same crew reported that a door in the back of the keepers' quarters that was kept locked at all times flew open with a bang nightly even on calm nights with little or no wind.

During the renovations, construction workers uncovered bloodstains on the pine floors in an upstairs room of the keepers' quarters. A dark blood splotch about one foot in length lays to the left of the fireplace. Another splatter lays to the right of the window. The bloodstains also dapple the floor from the doorway to a corner of the room where Lighthouse volunteers and military personnel believe lighthouse keepers' would have kept a bed.

Folklore about the bloodstains abounds. One story has it that an abusive relationship between a Lighthouse keeper and his wife came to a head in the 1880s when the wife became tired of her husband's abuse. According to the story, the couple was arguing in their bedroom. He lashed out as usual and struck her. She pulled a knife from her dress and stabbed him continuously as he flailed around the room trying to reach the bedroom door to escape. Another version of the story tells of a lonely and isolated keeper's wife, who, after years of desolate frustration, attacked and stabbed her husband to death in their bedroom.

The floors in the room, which now serve as a military office, have been sanded and refinished...but the stains still mark the floor. On humid summer days the stains become even more pronounced in spite of several coats of polyurethane sealer. Lighthouse volunteers say there is no record of a murder having taken place in that room. Military personnel and volunteers say that the bloodstains are most likely from childbirth, possibly Ella Miller's. But as one volunteer commented, "This is a military base. Records are kept [pause] differently." Volunteers say many who visit the Lighthouse comment that that room has an "evil feeling" or that the room makes them "feel nervous."

Lighthouse renovations were completed in 1995, but who or whatever was trying to get the workers attention has not rested in its efforts. Military personnel with offices in the keepers' quarters often hear footsteps on the second-floor porch and on the keepers' quarters' stairs and female voices echoing throughout the quarters when they know they are alone in the building.

Volunteers, visitors, and military personnel have also often described feeling "uneasy" or "watched" in the tower especially near the small room at the base that served as the keepers' quarters before the duplex home was built. Frequently visitors who request to climb the tower change their mind when they reach that area.

The basement of the keepers' quarters — the same place where renovation workers grappled with the infamous rope — is another area where Lighthouse volunteers and visitors frequently feel they are not alone. Volunteers often hear footsteps on the cellar stairs when there is no one else in the building. Dianne heard footsteps on the cellar stairs when she was closing up the Lighthouse alone one evening. She had looked down the cellar stairs to make sure that the light had been turned off and then heard heavy footsteps coming up the stairs as she was closing the door. She opened the door slightly in response and heard the footsteps pass though the cellar door, turn down the hallway, and walk straight through the front door of the keepers' quarters to the outside porch.

On another occasion, John Foote, a retired civilian, was in the basement cleaning and cataloging artifacts. A family

Visitors to the Pensacola Lighthouse have heard the disembodied voice of a gruff older man calling their name on the keepers' quarters stairs.

with a young boy was visiting the Lighthouse that day. As Dianne was talking to the boy's mother, the boy wandered down to the basement.

He soon returned and stood next to his mother and Dianne until he could get their attention. He said, "There is somebody down there." Dianne explained to him that John was in the basement cataloging artifacts. The boy said, "No, not him, the other man... the one in the back room." The mother explained to Dianne that they lived in an old house and that the boy seemed to have some sensitivity to spirits.

Chief Storekeeper Marylyn Warner often hears footsteps and senses movement on the second-floor porch from her desk.

"I hear someone walking around out there. It's always after the cleaning crew has left," says Marylyn. "I get up and look. I never see anyone."

Not everyone who has worked in the Pensacola Lighthouse over the years has been that lucky. As documented in the Travel Channel's "America's Most Haunted Places," at least one Lighthouse maintenance worker came face-to-face with a keeper from the past....

It was a dark, cold winter night. Two Navy plumbers were on the grounds checking the Lighthouse for frozen pipes. The lead plumber had walked around the Lighthouse four times. He decided to double check one of the pipes before he went home for the evening. When he bent down, he sensed someone walking behind him. He stood up and saw a man walking toward the front door of the keepers' quarters.

Thinking it was his partner, Ed, he called out, "Ed, are you just about done?" The man turned toward him and he realized immediately that the man walking toward the keepers' quarters was not Ed. He had a long white beard and was wearing a dark, wool coat and a captain's hat. The mysterious man looked at him and said, "I'll never be done."

On several occasions, visitors to the Lighthouse, and those enjoying the beach just steps away, have seen female and male apparitions in and around the Lighthouse. There have been several reports of people seeing ghostly figures in the Lighthouse windows. The male apparition is often described as looking "angry" or "mean."

Also documented in the Travel Channel special, in 1997, a family picnicking on the beach near the Lighthouse saw something very strange on the balcony of the tower. It was dusk and the family was packing up from a picnic on the beach in front of the Lighthouse. The daughter noticed the figure of a woman standing on the tower balcony. She told her mother what she had seen. Both of them stood on the beach watching as a woman with long, dark hair wearing a long white nightgown stood on the balcony looking out to sea as the beacon from the Lighthouse rhythmically passed through her transparent body.

One night, near midnight, the on-call officer, Coast Guardsman Ricky Pullen and his wife, Delaney, received a call at home that the Lighthouse light was not rotating. Ricky and Delaney arrived at the Lighthouse moments after receiving the call. As they approached the keepers' quarters, they heard noises on the other side of the door, inside the quarters. It sounded as if a man was stomping angrily around and grumbling under his breath. The couple entered the keepers' quarters and called out to the man, but no one answered. They walked through the keepers' quarters to the Lighthouse beam light switch. Ricky flipped the switch to restart the tower's light rotation. As he was standing by the switch, he felt and heard someone pacing back and forth bedside him.

The spirits of the Pensacola Lighthouse also made themselves known to a PBS film crew shooting a documentary about Florida lighthouses. A Coast Guard auxiliary member and a public affairs officer were leading the PBS crew through the keepers' quarters toward the command room.

One of the PBS crewmembers asked if the Lighthouse was haunted. Suddenly, as if to answer his question, the atmosphere of the room changed. The PBS crew and the officers looked to each other for confirmation of the heavy feeling that had settled in the room. The hair on everyone's arms and on the backs of their necks stood up. The solid mahogany door to the Lighthouse tower slammed shut by an unseen force.

Over the years, volunteers have given many tours of the Lighthouse to tourists, school children, and members of the media. During several of these tours, visitors and tour guides have had many unforgettable experiences.

During one tour, a Lighthouse guide was leading a group of people up the tower stairs when she felt a tap on her shoulder. She thought it was someone who needed her to move over so he or she could get down the steps. She turned in the direction of the tap, but there was no one there.

On another occasion, a young boy was walking down the tower stairs when he heard a man call his name. The boy's father, the only man in the quarters at the time, had not been calling him.

During another day of tours, a group of local school children was visiting the Lighthouse on a field trip. A tour guide was walking them through the keepers' quarters toward the command room, telling them about the history of the Lighthouse and the Naval Air Station. As they stood in the command room, the tour guide heard Coast Guard Yeoman, whose office was in the room above them, rolling his chair around behind his desk. The guide teased the children saying, "Is that the Lighthouse ghost I hear?" Suddenly, the door across from the tower flew open violently. Another visitor enjoying the tour was standing in same area when he felt an unseen force grab his camera strap and try to pull it from his shoulder.

On another occasion, two visitors were standing in a downstairs room in the keepers' quarters talking. They both sensed that they were not alone in the room, as the temperature in the room suddenly dropped several degrees. The hair on their arms and on the backs of their necks stood up.

Halloween of 1999 fell on a Sunday and the Lighthouse was open for tours. It was to be the last tour of the season and volunteers decided to get into the spirit of the holiday. They dressed in costumes and decorated the keepers' quarters and the entrance to the tower. A CD player in the old keepers' quarters in the Lighthouse tower played spooky music.

Throughout the night's tours, visitors commented separately that they felt a strange "chill" that made their hair stand on end when they passed by the former keepers' quarters room. Several people smelled pipe tobacco in the control room and in the Lighthouse tower.

During the evening two teenage girls wandered into the Lighthouse tower where the CD player was. As they walked into the room, a CD that was sitting on top of the CD player rose straight up into the air and then fell to the floor. The girls ran screaming from the room.

Also on that night, one of the tour guides was taking a small group of people up the tower stairs. She joked out loud, "Now, Mr. Ghost, please don't scare these nice people." Immediately, the guide felt three distinct taps on the back of her elbow.

"Everyone who spends any amount of time in the Lighthouse seems to have some type of experience," says Dianne. "This is one of the most haunted lighthouses in the country."

Civil War Union Camp Site/
Native American Burial Grounds

> "*I was sitting at the bottom of the stairs reading a magazine. I saw a white figure move across the room. I looked up and watched it move through the wall.*"
>
> -- Chandler M.,
> former resident

One of the many duplex homes built on the site of a Civil War Union Camp and Native American burial grounds on the Naval Air Station in Pensacola. Residents of these homes often see apparitions of men in uniform walking aimlessly in their homes.

The Pensacola Naval Air Station (NAS) is rich in history. There are areas on the base that people have inhabited since the early 1600s. Native American tribes, the Spanish, and the English all have fought each other and the deadly

The back yard of a duplex home at the site of a Civil War Union Camp on the Pensacola Naval Air Station. Civil War and Native American artifacts have been found in the front and backyards of the homes, which are believed to have been built on a Native American burial ground.

and heinous Yellow Fever disease to inhabit this land. Historical artifacts have been discovered on the base as recently as the late 1980s when an archaeological dig outside of a housing complex revealed the remains of a Civil War Union Camp.

Although area residents were excited to see the many artifacts unearthed at the site, including Civil War era bullets, pieces of antique weaponry, and even the site's mass burial ground for horses, which apparently fell victim to food shortages, those living in the duplexes surrounding the site and in the homes of the nearby Old Medical Complex were not surprised by the find. Residents and many visitors to this particular area of the base knew there were Union soldiers there long before the first archaeologist's shovel broke the ground.

The apparition of a Union Civil War soldier has been seen walking through the hallway of this home on the Pensacola Naval Air Station.

Residents of the homes that line the Union Civil War Camp site often see uniformed men in their peripheral vision wandering around their homes and grounds. Residents come home to find their doors unlocked and their kitchen cabinets open.

Jennifer M., a former resident of one of the many duplex homes that line the former Union Civil War Camp site, was standing in the kitchen of her home cooking dinner one evening when she heard someone walk in the front door. The uniformed man walked through the living room and past the kitchen door pausing for a moment to glance at Jennifer as he passed.

Assuming it was her husband, Jennifer called out to him. When she did not receive a response, she walked around the corner into the front room. There was no one in the front room and there would have been no way out without walking past her again.

"He was wearing some type of uniform," says Jennifer. "I could tell by the way his head was tilted that he was looking at me as he walked by."

On another occasion, Jennifer's sister was visiting for a few days. She was in a deep sleep on the living room couch when movement in the room suddenly awakened her. She opened her eyes and saw a man in a strange uniform walking around the room aimlessly just a few feet away from her. She watched him for a moment and then closed her eyes. When she opened them again, he was gone.

In the same home, Jennifer's son Chandler was sitting at the bottom of the stairs around midnight reading a magazine. There was a slight light illuminating the hallway from the stairs. He saw movement in his peripheral vision and then watched as a white shadowy figure moved across the room and through the living-room wall.

"I hauled it upstairs," says Chandler. "That was the last time I went downstairs at night."

On several nights around midnight, the door to Chandler's bedroom would push open by unseen hands. And the doors from the living room to the outside seemed to unlock by themselves.

"We would lock all of the doors at night before we went to bed. In the morning when we got up, all of the doors were unlocked," says Chandler.

"The doors just didn't stay locked in that house."

Rose, another area resident, experienced similar problems with her doors. She would often wake up in the morning or come home from work and find her cabinets, refrigerator, and microwave doors wide open.

At least one area resident had an experience that sent chills up his spine. He was in the attic storage area of his family's duplex clearing out their belongings in preparation for a move.

He became very uncomfortable and could not shake the feeling that someone was watching him. When he was finished, he gathered the last of their things and turned off the light on his way out. After he placed their belongings in his truck, he looked up at the storage unit where he was working moments before. The light was on and a very large male figure in uniform was standing at the window looking down at him.

Old Military Hospital Compound

In 1826 the first Naval hospital compound was established at the Pensacola Naval Air Station. Hospital compound facilities and medical-staff housing was surrounded by an eight-foot high wall, which many believe was constructed to block mosquitoes carrying the deadly Yellow Fever.

In 1826, just four years after Florida acquired Pensacola from Spain, the first Naval hospital was established at the Naval Air Station Pensacola (NAS). Hospital facilities and medical staff housing was surrounded by an eight-foot high wall, which many believe was constructed to stave off the mosquitoes they

Many of the duplex homes once housed hospital compound staff in the 1800s. Residents of the homes have seen Union Civil War soldiers walking toward their homes.

suspected were carrying the deadly Yellow Fever disease. The buildings of the old hospital compound now serve as residences for military personnel.

Several residents of the homes have seen Union Civil War soldiers walking around the grounds and have been terrorized at night by stomping footsteps and unexplained banging sounds.

An attorney who lived in one of the hospital compound homes came home for lunch every day. One day, while he was sitting in the kitchen eating, he noticed a man in an odd-looking uniform walking toward his home. He thought the man was a member of the maintenance staff and that if he needed to come in, he would knock on the door. Then, he saw the man again walking in the yard and realized he was wearing a Union Civil War soldier's uniform.

On another occasion, the attorney's sister and her family were visiting from Massachusetts. They had gone out for dinner. As they drove into the driveway, they saw a group of men dressed in Union Civil War uniforms walking together toward the house. They watched as the men walked straight across the courtyard toward the house and then...*faded out*.

Others living in the homes shared the same experience. They would see a man in a uniform walking in their peripheral vision and then turn to look just in time to see him fade away.

Jennifer and her family lived in one of the duplex homes of the old hospital compound. They say they were reminded of the history of the building the first night they arrived and almost every night after...as the sound of heavy boots stomping around the house would awaken them every night. They stomped down the hallway and to the edge of the bed like clockwork every two hours. When the stomping began, the family's otherwise docile dog would become extremely aggressive. It would crouch down as if it were going to attack something, bare its teeth, and growl. The dog would then launch itself from under the bed and run down the hallway toward the dining room.

"It sounded like a man wearing heavy boots," says Jennifer. "It happened the first night we were there. I just never slept. I'd calm myself down and then it would start again."

On other nights the family was awakened by what sounded like a two-by-four being slammed into the dining room wall.

"We would hear it slamming and go in there and there would be nothing there and no damage.

"I was scared of it. I wanted it out. I just wanted to sleep."

After months of missed sleep, and at the urging of a priest, Jennifer decided to recite a prayer to the entity as it was stomping toward her bed. As soon as she recited the prayer, it stopped. The family thought the problem had been solved. But the next night, they heard the footsteps through the ceiling as the presence stomped between the children's rooms on the second floor. For the rest of their stay in the home, every night the entity stomped down the hallway between the upstairs bedrooms and jiggled the doorknobs. The resident of the duplex next door to the family said she could hear the stomping and the banging through the walls.

"My sons were afraid to go to the bathroom," says Jennifer.

On one occasion, Jennifer's brother came for a visit. He was sleeping on the couch in the living room. Throughout the night he heard male voices carrying on conversations in the dining room. In the morning, he asked if anyone had been up talking. Everyone in the house had gone to sleep when he did.

One day the neighbors gathered together to enjoy a cookout in the backyard of the homes. Jennifer and the woman who lived in the duplex next door were discussing the nightly stomping and the banging sounds in the duplex. One of the women attending the cookout noticed that there was a woman wearing a long, white dress standing off by herself watching them. She looked away for a moment and the woman was gone.

The Homes of Admiral's Row

Building A of Admiral's Row on the Pensacola Naval Air Station has been housing Admirals since 1874. Residents of the homes have seen the apparition of lady in a long, white dress walking with a little boy.

Admiral's Row on the Naval Air Station Pensacola (NAS) is an area of housing along the waterfront for military personnel that dates back to the early 1800s. Building A of the Row is infamous among NAS personnel as a place steeped in the folklore of Commodore William B. Woolsey, who died of Yellow Fever in the home. Residents of the homes in the area say that whatever haunts Admiral's Row seems to travel from one home to another.

Many of the foundations of the homes on Admiral's Row were constructed in the 1820s to support buildings of the Fort Barrancas Naval Yard.

In 2004, Hurricane Ivan destroyed several of the homes of Admiral's Row. Military personnel decided they were beyond repair and leveled them to their foundations. The few homes that remain stand stoically next to original stone walkways that now lead to grassy open lots.

Residents of these stately homes have seen the apparition of a woman in a long, white dress or nightgown walking about the hallways of their homes. The "lady in white," as area residents call her, is often seen walking with a young boy. Residents have also seen a man wearing a military uniform standing in the living room of one of the homes. There are doors that will not remain closed or locked, and doors that slam shut by unseen hands.

The Robbins family lived in Building C of Admiral's Row. Family members learned the first day they moved to the Row that they would be *sharing* their new home with someone or something unseen. The Robbins' teenage daughter and the family dog were the first to encounter something strange in the house. They arrived at the home on moving day before the rest of the family. The Robbins' daughter began to move her belongings into the home. Several times she heard footsteps on the wooden floors in the hallways and on the staircase.[6]

She stopped to listen. Suddenly, all of the bedroom doors slammed shut at the same time. The dog started to growl and bared its teeth. The hair stood up on its back. She left the home, but had to leave the dog that was continuing to growl and refused to leave. When the Robbins family returned to the home later that day, all of the bedroom doors were closed.[6]

On several occasions, family members saw the lady in white. One evening, the Robbins were having a party. Guests were visiting in the living room and in the kitchen. One of the guests approached Mrs. Robbins to ask her the name of the woman standing alone in the living room. The guest described her as a very proper looking woman wearing a long, white dress; she seemed out of place and disconnected from the party. When Mrs. Robbins went to the living room to investigate, the woman was gone. On another occasion, the Robbins' daughter watched in awe as the lady in white walked across the home's dining room and into the butler's pantry.[6]

The Pruits family also lived in a home on Admiral's Row. The first night the Pruits stayed in their new home, their son complained that the lights would not turn off in his room. They turned the lights off in his room several times during the night. Moments later they came back on. Eventually they unplugged them.

The Pruitts also had difficulty with a door at the end of the home's back hallway that led to the backyard. The door would not stay locked. Family members continuously locked the door and checked the lock only to find it unlocked and open moments later.

"In the two and half years we lived in that house, that door was never shut," said Lisa Pruitt. "It didn't matter how many times we shut and locked it...it was open."

Sherri, another resident of a home on Admiral's Row, was downstairs when she heard furniture sliding across the floor in the rooms above her. She went upstairs and found that the French doors that had been painted shut were opening and closing by themselves.

Among the homes of Admiral's Row is an octagonal-shaped building constructed in 1834 that once served as an officers' club. For years, officers on the base gathered there to play cards. The building is now office space. Many who work in the building have reported hearing the sounds of poker chips falling on a wooden table. Legend has it that Marine Captain Guy Hall, who often played poker in the building in the 1920s, had a habit of picking up his poker chips and dropping them on the table.

Although many of the homes of Admiral's Row seem to be inhabited by residents of the past, Building A is by far the most notorious. The home burned to the ground during the Civil War and was rebuilt in 1874 for Commodore William B. Woolsey, a man who was so invested in the home's refurbishing that he traveled to New York so he could choose the fireplace mantels and the woodwork for the windows and the doors.

The folklore that surrounds the death of Commodore Woolsey is just one story of thousands of people who lived during the misery that Yellow Fever brought to the coast of Florida in the 1700s and 1800s. The disease that shut down its victims' kidneys, turned their skin yellow, and caused vomiting, abdominal pain, and bleeding from the eyes and mouth ravaged the United States, killing more than 15,000 people along the Gulf Coast alone.

Although rightly blamed for its spread, health professionals did not know for sure that mosquitoes carried the deadly disease until the 1900s. One belief, albeit misguided, was that mosquitoes that carried the disease could not fly higher than eight feet. One version of the folklore that surrounds Commodore Woolsey is that he took solace in this belief and locked himself and his beloved cat in the cupola of Building A.

The Commodore had his food and drink, including a daily rum beverage that he believed offered him further protection from illness, hoisted to him with a pulley. As the story goes, one day his servants forgot to include his rum and soon after the Commodore became ill with Yellow Fever and died. Another version of the story has it that the Commodore's servants and mistress dutifully provided his food and beverages to him until one by one they all succumbed to Yellow Fever. The Commodore was too crippled with fear to leave the cupola and he and his cat languished in the copula eventually dying of dehydration.

Residents and guests of Building A have reported the feeling of being followed; strong odors including flowery perfume and smoke and pipe tobacco; doors slamming shut from unseen forces; and the sounds of people moving about on the third floor when there is no one staying there. The lady in white has been seen walking casually about on the third floor with the apparition of a young boy.

An Admiral who was alone in the home one evening came home from work and walked into the house through the back door. As he was walking through the kitchen and the dining room he heard the sounds of a dress swishing in the foyer. He followed the noise into the foyer. Then he heard it again. It sounded as if someone wearing a heavy dress with petticoats was walking up the stairs. He followed the sound up the stairs to the second floor, but he could not find its source.[6]

Residents of Building A often are awakened in the night by strange sounds and smells. One Admiral staying in the home alone was awakened by the sound of glass shattering. He inspected the home, but could not find anything broken. On another night, he and his wife were awakened in the middle of the night by an overwhelming smell of smoke that had permeated their bedroom. The fire department inspected the home and the surrounding area, but could not find the source of the odor.

One Admiral's wife, who lived in the home, complained that she could not keep a flower arrangement on the dining room table. Each time she set a flower arrangement or centerpiece on the table, unseen hands moved it the moment she left the room. A close friend of one of the residents of the home also had a first-hand experience with the moving centerpieces. She had come to the home to help decorate for Christmas. She placed a holiday-themed flower arrangement on the dining room table and walked out of the room. Moments later, when she returned to the room, the arrangement had been pushed to the side.[5]

Residents and guests of the home often see the apparition of an elderly lady clutching a handkerchief to her mouth and the apparition of a man many believe is the ghost of Commodore Woolsey. Some have even had an encounter with the Commodore's cat.

A mess specialist was alone in the home working in the living room on a maintenance project. He sensed that someone was standing behind him. He turned around and found himself face-to-face with a man dressed in the military regalia of a senior officer of the 1800s. As the mess specialist moved away from the man, the man disappeared.[6]

On another occasion, an Admiral's wife was sitting in the parlor talking to her sister on the phone when she noticed movement on the front staircase. She looked up and watched in shock as an elderly woman in a white dress clutching a scarf to her face walked toward her. The apparition disappeared before it reached her.[5]

Although there are odd occurrences in almost every area of Building A, residents say it's the third floor of the home, which leads to the cupola, that seems to have the greatest activity.

Guests and workers on the third floor report feeling that someone is watching them. Residents say they often hear footsteps and movement on that floor when there is no one staying there.

A mess specialist working on the third floor heard the bedroom television on the second floor turn on and play very loudly. He walked down the stairs to tell who ever it was that he was working on the third floor. When he reached the room, the television was blaring through the door. He knocked on the door several times, but did not get an answer. He opened the door slightly and called out, "Hello." No one answered. He walked into the room, turned the television off, and called out again, but got no answer.[5]

The specialist returned to the third floor and began working again. Moments later he heard the television again blasting loudly through the home. He walked back down the stairs to the second-floor bedroom. He turned off the television and walked to the garage to check that the family car was not in the driveway. When he was sure that he was alone in the home, he decided to wait on the first floor for the homeowners to return.[6]

The Wrights lived in Admiral's Row for several years and had many experiences on the home's third floor. When Dixie and Harry Wright moved into the home, one of the first things Dixie did was close and latch the door that leads to the home's cupola. She showed the home often and did not feel comfortable with people walking up and down the thin, winding stairs that led to the cupola. She soon realized that no matter how many times she shut and locked the cupola, when she returned to the third floor, the door would be unlocked and open.

"I thought it wasn't latching," said Dixie. "I kept checking it and relocking it and then I finally just said out loud, 'Okay, you win' and left it open."

Shortly after they moved into the home, some family friends came for a visit. They stayed in one of the third-floor guest rooms. At breakfast, one of the guests commented that she enjoyed the cat that had slept on her bed with her the night before. She said the cat had curled up at her feet and purred for most of the night.

Dixie replied, "We don't have a cat. But have you ever heard of a man named Commodore Woolsey?"

The same guest commented that the hair dryer she kept wrapped up in its cord on the bathroom counter was always unwound when she returned to the bathroom. Sometimes it was unwound only moments after she had wrapped it and placed it on the counter.

Just before Christmas, Dixie had laid out her collection of angels on the cupola stairs for holiday decorating. She and her family left to attend a party. When she returned to the cupola, all of the angels were laying on their sides. None of them were broken.

"It was as if someone had just gently laid them one by one on their sides," says Dixie.

That Christmas the Wrights' extended family filled the home. There were twenty-six people staying in the house, many of them in the third-floor guest rooms. Dixie didn't mention any of the stories about Admiral's Row to her family. She didn't want anyone to be afraid to stay in the home. Among the guests were Dixie's niece and nephew and their three-month old baby.

Dixie's nephew went up to the third floor to put the baby down for a nap. As he was walking down the hallway to their room, he saw the apparitions of a woman in a long, white dress walking down the hallway with a little boy. He quickly came back downstairs with the baby.

"He was very white faced," says Dixie. "We thought he was teasing us at first. But...he was so scared. He didn't go to the third floor by himself for the rest of the visit."

"I'm a believer," says Dixie. "I don't think they are mean. The ones we had were not mean at all."

The Billingsley House
Woolsey & Warrington Cemetery

The Billingsley House was built in the 1920s on the land of the former Woolsey and Warrington Cemetery. The United States military moved more than seven hundred graves from the early settlements to make room for needed construction.

The Billingsley House on the Naval Air Station Pensacola (NAS) was one of many homes built on the base in the 1920s to accommodate the growing military. With limited land to build on, NAS management decided to build on the site of the former towns of Woolsey and Warrington, two of Pensacola's first settlements. To do so, NAS had to relocate more than seven hundred graves at the old Woolsey and Warrington Cemetery.

The towns of Woolsey and Warrington were established in the 1820s when the United States Navy hired civilian craftsmen to help construct Navy ships. At the time, the remote naval yard was accessible only by horse or boat.

Commanding Officer Captain Lewis Warrington and Captain Melanchton T. Woolsey requested permits to construct housing near the yard for the workers and their families. Workers were permitted to settle either to the west or to the north of the yard. Soon there were general merchandise stores, a meat market, a blacksmith shop, and eventually the cemetery. The village to the west of the yard was named Warrington; the village to the north was named Woolsey.

The graves of the Warrington and Woolsey villagers were unearthed and relocated to the Pensacola National Cemetery. Although NAS workers did their best to move all of the coffins and headstones, occasionally during a fierce storm, a missed headstone pushes up through the rain-soaked ground. In 2004, when Hurricane Ivan pummeled the base, the headstone of a forgotten grave popped up from beneath a toppled tree just a few feet away from the Billingsley House.

The Billingsley House is a large three-story home with sprawling living quarters on the main level and cozy bedrooms on the second floor. The home's attic is a large open room with hardwood floors that, for some families, served as a spacious children's playroom. Residents of the Billingsley House report strange noises coming from the attic, including footsteps and the sounds of a child's ball rolling and bouncing on the wooden floor of the attic. Billingsley residents and neighbors have also seen the apparition of a blond-haired woman in a long, blue dress walking about the halls and standing on the second-level front porch.

Late one evening, resident Jim M. was carrying the family's new puppy, Rascal, out to the front yard at 2 a.m. on a brightly moonlit night. He was standing in the yard while the puppy wandered about, sniffing the grass. He noticed movement in the home in his peripheral vision and looked up to see what he believed to be his wife, Jennifer, walk down the home's front staircase and then turn to walk into the kitchen. When Rascal was finished, Jim followed the woman into the kitchen and called out to her, but there was no one there.

When he returned to the bedroom, he found Jennifer fast asleep just as she had been when he left her.

"She came down the stairs and walked really casually toward the kitchen," says Jim. "I was never a believer in ghosts. But I thought, 'okay... now I have seen something I can't explain.'

"I didn't just see a figure. I saw that woman walking toward the kitchen."

On another occasion, Jennifer was carrying Rascal down the stairs to go outside at 3 a.m. She scooped up Rascal and was walking down the stairs without stopping to turn on the lights. At the bottom of the stairs, Jennifer became overwhelmed with a feeling that she was not alone.

"I got to the floor and I felt like something was right on my neck," Jennifer says. "I kept thinking, 'don't look; just don't look; just keep walking.' I flipped on the light and ran outside as fast as I could.

"I've never felt that way before."

One early evening the family's fifteen-year-old son, Jimmy, was walking down the sidewalk with a friend. It was dusk and the light of the day was just starting to darken. As they walked up the sidewalk toward the Billingsley House they saw a blond-haired woman they assumed was Jimmy's mother standing on the second-story front porch.

They called out, "Mom, what are you doing?" But the woman did not respond. They continued to playfully yell at her to get her attention, getting sillier and louder as they got closer to the house. Then they noticed that the blond-haired woman who was staring blankly out from the porch was not Jennifer. As they walked closer to the house... *she became transparent and faded away*.

Billingsley residents often set squirrel and rat traps in unsuccessful attempts to capture whatever was making the sounds of balls rolling in the attic. Residents are often awakened at night by the sounds of footsteps in the attic and of people talking. Maintenance workers have been called to investigate the odd noises that seem to only emanate from the attic in the quiet of night, but none have been able to find the source of the noises.

"Some nights we would lay in our beds and listen to what sounded like a child's ball rolling and bouncing on the hardwood floor of the attic right above our heads," says Jennifer.

Courtesy of Pensacola CVB.

3

Pensacola

Ten thousand years ago Pensacola's wilderness was home to many tribes of Native Americans. In 1559, the first European set foot on the land in the first of many attempts to colonize the area and establish a port for trade and exploration.

Spanish explorer Don Tristán de Luna y Arellano arrived in the area with thousands of soldiers, farmers, metalworkers, and priests in tow only to be met by a vicious hurricane that destroyed their ships and supplies.

In 1698, the Spanish tried again. Explorer Don Andres d'Arriola successfully established the city of Pensacola. They lost the colony to the French one year later when the Governor of the recently established Louisiana was ordered by the French monarchy to invade and capture the city.

France and Spain continued to squabbled over the city, burning it to the ground several times. In 1772, Pensacola was restored to Spain and by 1763 the city was well established. The United States gained possession of the city in 1821 and then lost it in 1860 when Florida seceded from the Union. Following the Civil War, the area grew steadily with the building of railroads and became a modern community.[7]

Pensacola Little Theatre

> "*I had to go to costume storage under the stage. I walked into the back room. There were racks and racks of clothes. I felt something looking at me. Then I saw her — a little girl standing there looking at me with a half smile. Her hair was in perfect Victorian ringlets.*"
>
> -- Carol Kahn Parker,
> Pensacola Little Theatre volunteer

PENSACOLA CULTURAL CENTER

In the early 1900s, the building that houses the Pensacola Little Theatre served as the county sheriff's office and the county jail. Considered state-of-the-industry for its time, all of the cells faced the gallows.

he Pensacola Little Theatre is a lively, energetic place with a creative energy that seems to seep out from its doors and into the city outside. Jovial actors, staff, and volunteers talk excitedly about future performances. Light-hearted conversation and laughter seem to permeate the halls and rooms of the old building. It is hard to believe that the structure once was a place of grave consequences, pain, and death.

The Theatre that now welcomes thousands of Pensacola residents and tourists to performances of "The Glass Menagerie" and "The Wizard of Oz" once served as the county jail and execution facility. Small cube-like cells housing murderous inmates lined the walls of the building that now contains the stage, audience seating, and a technical booth. Theatre patrons enjoy intermission snacks in the atrium, a place where inmates once were hanged for their crimes. And years before that, the British doled out their public punishments of flogging, tar and feathering, and the use of the pillory and stocks on the same land.[8]

In the early 1900s, the Pensacola Little Theatre building served as the County Court of Record. The building was separated into two sections with one side housing court facilities, judge chambers, and the office of the sheriff.[3] The other side of the building housed the county jail. Considered state-of-the-industry for its time, all of the cells faced the gallows.[3] The jail and court continued to operate in the building until 1955 when a new facility was constructed on Leonard Street. The building was stripped of its contents and remained empty until it was deeded to the Pensacola Little Theatre in 1998.[8]

Theatre staff, volunteers, and actors have seen apparitions of a little girl in the basement and the auditorium, and a dark shadowy man throughout the building. Actors are routinely locked in dressing rooms by unseen hands. Staff is especially leery of going to the costume storage area in the basement by themselves. Costume storage is at the end of a *long*, gray hallway in the back corner of a larger storage room with dark concrete walls. Volunteers and staff say that these rooms –

Patrons of the Pensacola Little Theatre enjoy intermission snacks in the atrium, where inmates once were hanged for their crimes. Years earlier, the British doled out their public punishments of flogging, tar, and feathering and the use of the pillory and stocks on the land.

Volunteers working in Pensacola Little Theatre's technical booth have seen apparitions float by the window. One staff member was locked in the booth by unseen hands.

and the hallway that leads to them – are the most haunted areas in the Theatre.

The small costume storage room is lit by a single light bulb and the switch is far removed from the room. Those who are brave enough to go into the room alone often find themselves standing in complete blackness. Making their way out of the room, they'll find that the light switch was turned off...yet there is no one else in the basement.

Katie, an actress who was performing at the Theatre, was walking down the basement hallway toward the costume storage area. She heard someone moving quickly behind her and moved to get out of the way. She felt a strong, cold

Actors and volunteers at the Pensacola Little Theatre have seen the apparition of a young girl dressed in Victorian-style clothing as well as a "dark looking" man lurking quietly in the basement.

swoosh of air move past her, but yet…there was no one else in the hallway.

Theatre committee member Donna Holt was in the costume storage room looking through the racks. She heard muffled male voices that sounded as if they were coming from the large storage room just outside of the door. She called out, "Hey," and walked toward the noise. There was no one in the large storage room or the hallway.

Another volunteer was walking down the basement hallway toward the storage rooms. He walked into the darkness of the large storage room and reached for the light switch. As his hand fumbled on the wall for the light switch, his eyes began to adjust to the darkness. He saw a large, dark shadowy man standing in front of him. He opened his mouth to speak and the man disappeared. Many volunteers have seen children playing in their peripheral vision and have heard the sounds of small footsteps running on the concrete and giggling in the hallway.

"There is a lot of activity here that cannot be explained," says Rodney Walker, a Theatre committee member. "There are some people who won't go into the basement at all and many more who won't go down there alone."

One volunteer, who did not know about the activity in the Theatre's basement, was working in the costume storage room organizing the costume racks. She heard the sounds of children laughing and running in the hallway. Several times she looked out the door and saw them running in the larger storage room and in the hallway in her peripheral vision. The lights were switched off and she had to make her way to the outer room with her arms outstretched in the dark, still hearing the sounds of children giggling in the hallway. When she couldn't find any children hiding in the large storage room or in the hallway, she decided to go back upstairs.

Actors and volunteers often hear children's laughter in the costume storage room in the Theatre's basement.

One evening, volunteer Carol Kahn Parker went to the basement by herself to retrieve a costume piece for a performer. She walked through the rows of costumes in the tiny room, digging through the mounds of clothes. She sensed that she was not alone. She turned toward the door of the storage room and saw a little girl standing by one of the racks smiling at her. She was wearing a Victorian-style dress and her hair was in ringlets around her face.

The basement is not the only area in the Theatre where the playful young girl has been spotted. The little girl has also been seen sitting in the auditorium during performances.

One patron reported to volunteers that she had seen a little girl in the auditorium sitting by herself who didn't seem to fit. It was a very well sold show and the auditorium was almost full. The woman noticed a very well-dressed little girl sitting alone a few rows ahead of her. The little girl glanced back at her and smiled several times throughout the first half of the show. When the lights turned on at intermission, the seat was empty.

"We don't know who she is," says Rodney. "She seems to only be encountered on the first floor. She may be associated with the land before this building existed."

On at least one occasion, the apparition of a man has been seen on the auditorium stage. During an evening performance, an actor who was doing a solo scene noticed that there was a man wearing a white shirt and khaki pants standing on the stage to his right staring out at the audience. No one seemed to notice the man. When the performance was over, the actor looked over and the man was gone.

Several of the Theatre's staff and volunteers have heard disembodied voices in the elevator. The elevator buttons light up seconds before they are touched. Volunteers often have the sensation that something is standing behind them. One evening Donna stepped onto the elevator. She felt the presence of something very close to her ear...and then she heard someone whisper the word "whisper" in her ear. On another evening, Rodney stepped into the empty elevator and, as the doors were closing, heard a very clear voice say, "Hello."

Volunteers say it can be a great challenge to prepare for performances. Props that are carefully set up and laid out the night before are moved or are missing in the morning. Ropes and wires become tangled within moments of being set. During a performance of "Peter Pan," the rope to hoist an actor was set up and functioning properly moments before the show began, but during the performance, it became tangled and the actor fell to the stage.

"Cords are constantly being unplugged by unseen hands," says Rodney. "We do our best to arrange cords in a way that they cannot be snagged on anything and be unplugged. But...moments later they are tangled and unplugged.

"Sometimes we have to crawl under other props and move things out of the way to plug them back in."

In addition to props moving, cords unplugging, and ropes tangling, volunteers and actors often find doors that were just locked are now unlocked and doors that were just unlocked are locked. Actors and volunteers regularly find themselves locked in rooms. Actors were getting locked in the dressing rooms so often between scenes that staff had to remove all of the locks from the dressing room doors. Removing the locks seems to have solved the problem, even though the locking apparatuses were never set up to lock from the outside.

"It always seemed to happen moments before they needed to be onstage," says Rodney. "Someone would go looking for them and they'd be locked in the dressing room."

Although no one has been locked in the dressing room since the locks were removed, at least one staff member has been locked in the technology booth. Jennifer Godwin, a Theatre teacher, was in the technology booth in the auditorium. The small room does not have a locking door. When she tried to turn the doorknob to leave, it would not turn. Outside of the door she could hear heavy footsteps that sounded like they were walking on wood floors. The floors surrounding the technology booth are carpeted. After several minutes, another staff member walked by and opened the door.

Volunteers have also seen apparitions from the auditorium technology booth. On one occasion, Rodney was in the booth alone working on the soundboard. He was looking down at the equipment when he saw something move in front of the room in his peripheral vision. He looked up to see a dark shadow in the shape of a man floating past the booth window. The booth window is more than twelve feet off the ground.

"It was shaped like a human," Rodney says. "At that height, it would had to have been levitating."

The Unity Church of Pensacola

"I saw a dark figure rising out of a pew to my left. I thought it was a homeless person at first. But then it moved really fast through the pews as if they weren't there and disappeared. There was no sound."

-- Jamie Sanders,
Unity Church Reverend

The Unity Church of Pensacola is a warm, welcoming place that encourages people of all backgrounds and religious beliefs to come together to connect with God, whom Unity Church Reverend Jamie Sanders believes is "the hub" at the center of all of the world's religions. Jamie became the spiritual leader of the Unity Church in 2003. He describes his vision as empowering individuals to become more than they ever believed they could be.

Unity Church truly is a place of free-thinking spirituality. However, the building that houses the church has not always been a place of free thought and lively, thunderous music. The Sacred Heart Catholic Church of Pensacola constructed the church building in 1900. It was leveled by a tropical storm that same year and was rebuilt in 1906.

The church was one of many buildings Sacred Heart owned on the block including a rectory and a school. The original stained-glass windows from the 1906 reconstruction, with the names of the Sacred Heart patrons who funded them, still filter colorful beams of light into the chapel. The windows were crafted in Belgium and shipped to Pensacola five years before the building was rebuilt. Jamie and many church patrons believe that their church is special in that there are many patrons who have since passed on from life...*but still come to Unity Church to commune with God*.

The church that now houses the Unity Church of Pensacola was built in 1900 as a home for the original Sacred Heart Catholic Church. It was leveled by a tropical storm that same year and rebuilt in 1906. Church staff and patrons have seen the apparitions of a Native American woman and a sea captain in the sanctuary.

Reverend Sanders of the Unity Church of Pensacola witnessed a "black shadowy man" rise from the pews of his church and move quickly away from him through the pews.

Church staff often hear footsteps on the wood floors outside of their offices. Doorknobs rattle and turn seemingly by themselves so often that they rarely get up to check them anymore. Staff and patrons have seen ghostly apparitions walking in the church basement, peeking in the windows of the sanctuary entrance, and

Patrons of Unity Church have seen the apparitions of a Native American woman and a man described as a sea captain standing in the church entrance way. Pensacola psychic Sharon René visited the church and described a man standing on the sanctuary balcony wearing a dark jacket.

peering down at them from the sanctuary balcony. Dark shadowy figures have been seen springing up from the pews.

"You can feel the energy change when they are around," says Jamie.

"When the sound shifts in my ear, I start looking... Some people come in and immediately feel good energy."

One of the more common occurrences is the doorknob to the church office will turn and shake even though no one is on the other side of the door.

"We used to get up and check them," says Jamie, "but it happens so often. You get up to check on the door and it stops. As soon as you walk away, another one starts shaking."

Aside from the slightly unsettling shaking and rattling doorknobs he tried to ignore, it wasn't long before Jamie realized that he was never really alone in the church. One Saturday night, he was listening to music with his eyes closed in the sanctuary. When he opened his eyes, he immediately noticed the image of a man walking behind him reflected in the two-way mirror at the back of the sanctuary.

Jamie turned around to greet the man...*there was no one behind him*.

Confused, he looked again at the mirror and saw the man walking toward the double doors that led to the outside entrance to the sanctuary. The man was wearing a dark jacket. He had black, curly hair, thick and long sideburns, and a high collar.

"His clothing didn't look current," says Jamie. "It freaked me out. I thought someone had come into the building. When I realized I could only see him in the reflection, I knew what I was seeing.

"He walked right past me. When you see something like that, you wonder if you should even tell anyone."

One evening, Jamie decided to spend the night in his office rather than drive to his home in Fort Walton Beach and then back again in the morning to attend an early meeting. He was laying on the couch in his office with a pillow over his face trying to fall asleep, when he heard the wooden steps outside of his office door squeak and crack as if someone was walking from the sanctuary to his office. He lay there frozen for a moment and then heard a very distinct voice in his head whisper, "Are you sure you want to open your eyes?"

Jamie kept his eyes closed and said aloud, "You are not welcome in this space." Then he started to pray.

"There was some kind of energy in the room," said Jamie. "It used to frighten me, now I find it fascinating."

On New Year's Eve, Jamie was working late at the computer in his office when he again heard footsteps on the wood floor outside of his office door.

He got up, opened the door, and looked down the hallway into the sanctuary. There was no one there. Jamie went back to work at his desk. Almost immediately he felt the presence of something standing behind him. Again, he closed his eyes and said out loud, "*I told you...YOU are not welcome in this space.*" As he said it, he felt a "whoosh" and the feeling was gone.

"It was that same feeling I had when I slept in the office that night," says Jamie. "It's almost as if they are curious."

Jamie recently participated in a radio show from his office. The door from his office to the sanctuary was open. In the middle of the show, the door suddenly slammed shut.

One evening, Jamie was walking through the sanctuary on his way to the stairs that lead to the basement classrooms, where he was teaching a class that evening. The light filtering through the stained-glass windows was just beginning to fade. As he walked down the aisle, something "dark and shadowy" raised out of a pew to his right. Jamie watched as the dark figure rose from the pew and then darted from him as if he had startled it. It moved with an unusual speed passing right through the wooden pews.

"When it started to move," says Jamie, "I thought it was a real person. I thought it was a homeless person. But then it ran through the pews and there was no sound. I started to pray."

All during the classes that night, Jamie and his students could hear creaking and walking on the sanctuary floor above them. Several times students went up to check the room, but there was no one there.

On another evening, Jamie was walking through the sanctuary toward the double doors that lead to the street. He noticed a woman looking through the glass door. She looked Native American with straight, dark hair parted in the middle of her head and pulled tight on either side of her face. He thought it was strange that she was standing there expressionless staring in his direction. As he got closer to her, the image faded.

"At first I thought, 'that woman looks like Cher," said Jamie. "The closer I got to her, the more I felt that something was different about her. I felt compelled to walk toward her."

One night, several ladies were gathered in the Church for choir practice. As they walked through the sanctuary to go home for the night, they saw a man on the other side of the double doors dressed in a dark coat. They described him as looking "out of place" and "resembling a sea captain." As they approached the door, the man *faded* from view.

Several other patrons have described seeing a woman and a man walking on the balcony of the Church. During one Easter Sunday service several attendees saw the woman many described as Native American-looking standing on the sanctuary balcony. The balcony is not open to the public for safety reasons. The door that accesses the balcony is kept locked at all times.

Local psychic Sharon René visited the Church and described a man standing on the sanctuary balcony wearing a dark jacket. Sharon said he was asking where his dog was. Jamie knew immediately what she was talking about. A musical couple from Nashville with a small dog had visited the Church several times over the years. While the couple performed, the dog would sit beside them and stare into the balcony cocking its head from side to side.

Sharon also said a previous Church sexton appeared to her and told her that he was concerned that staff had forgotten to blow out the candles at night several times. The sexton commented that there had been a lot of changes in the Church, but that he liked them.

Rodney Walker, a sound technician for Unity Church, says he often hears "Yes" or "Rod" whispered into his ear when a song comes to an end...even though he is wearing headphones.

Many Church members describe feeling an energy in the basement at the bottom of the stairs. Staff recently discovered a room beneath the stairs that had been sealed off. They are not sure what the room was used for or why it was sealed. The only contents were newspapers from the 1950s and a few symphony programs. The room has since been resealed.

"The ladies tell me they feel 'creepy' using the ladies room in the basement," says Jamie. "One Church member says she heard something whisper 'sweet nothings' in her ear as she was using the facilities.

"I don't mind them being here," Jamie adds. "I don't think the congregation does either. But I am curious why they don't leave."

One early Sunday morning, Jamie went down to the basement and flipped on the lights. As the lights were flickering on, he saw the shape of a person walking in the room at the end of the hallway.

"I just assumed that one of the kids had beaten me here. It looked like he was stepping out of the way so I could come in," he said.

Jamie recently conducted a sermon called "Bring on the Rain" that addressed dealing with the pain of extreme loss. He incorporated the song by Jo Dee Messina and Tim McGraw. Jamie had advertised the sermon on his web site and locally in Pensacola.

A family called and told him that their daughter had just died and that that was her favorite song. Jamie dedicated the sermon to her. As they played the song in the sanctuary, all of the lights hanging down from the ceiling began to gently sway with the music.

"Everyone felt her presence," said Jamie.

"I've never felt meanness or felt threatened by what's here," says Jamie. "I do sometimes ask that they try not to scare me. This building is over a hundred years old now. It has been saturated with prayers.

"The bible says, 'In my Father's House, there are many mansions.' Before I came to Unity Church, I took that passage literally, but now I think it's talking about dimensions of being."

Pensacola Historical Museum

> *"There is a smell that you just can't put your finger on. It's not musty. It's decrepit. Something up there moves around. You see it out of the corner of your eye."*
> -- Wendi Davis, Curator of Exhibits, Pensacola Historical Museum

The building that houses the Pensacola Historical Museum was built in 1885 to serve sea-faring visitors and local workers as a saloon. It was a violent place where young men were shanghaied into forced labor on fishing boats. Museum staff see movement in their peripheral vision and experience odd sensations and smells in the building.

The Pensacola Historical Society offers visitors a museum with rich exhibits that capture the life and history of Pensacola. It even offers haunted walking and trolley

The second floor of the Pensacola Historical Museum is a place where visitors can view treasures from Pensacola's past. Visitors have seen the apparition of a young boy in Victorian-style clothing near the storage room at the end of the hall.

Pensacola Historical Museum staff often find children's books that were stowed away on shelves the night before laying on the floor in the morning. The book *Life as a Slave Girl* is found on the Museum Shop floor often.

tours of the historic city as an annual fundraiser, but what the museum staff don't often tell visitors is that Pensacola's history lives on in ways more than just its well-organized historical displays.

The building that houses the Museum was built in 1885 to serve sea-faring visitors and local workers as a saloon, an often violent place where young men were shanghaied into forced labor on fishing boats. Owner Eugenio Arbona and his family lived above the saloon. During the building's renovations, workers uncovered the body of an unknown man buried in the courtyard. He was likely the victim of a barroom brawl.

Museum staff say they often see movement in their peripheral vision and experience odd sensations and smells in the building— especially on the second floor, where the Arbona family lived.

"A lot of people come down from the upstairs in a hurry," says Wendi Davis, curator of exhibits. "Some say they will never go up there again. People find it especially uncomfortable at the end of the hall near the door to the storage room."

Several visitors to the museum have seen the apparition of a young boy wearing Victorian-style clothing at the end of the upstairs hallway. Visitors and staff smell a musty, "decrepit"

Museum staff hear footsteps on the stairs that lead to the second floor when there is no one else in the building. They also hear the sounds of furniture being slid across the wood floors.

odor that emanates from that floor. Other strange smells and unexplained odors occur on the first floor. Doors to the elevator that takes visitors from the gift shop area to the upstairs exhibits often open when the mechanical apparatus is locked.

The staff hear footsteps on the stairs that lead to the second floor when there is no one else in the building. They also hear the sounds of furniture being slid across the wood floors.

In the Museum Store, items are often moved by unseen hands. The staff will straighten the shop each night before they leave. Yet they often find that, when they return in the morning, books and toys have been knocked down or left on the floor.

"The children's books are moved most often," says Wendi. "Books from the children's bookshelf are often found piled on the floor as if someone had been reading them."

Intriguingly enough, staff find the book, *Life As A Slave Girl*, on the floor most often.

Pensacola Historical Village

> "*I never believed in ghosts until I started volunteering here. You hear so many stories. Nothing compares to when you feel your own hair stand up on end.*"
> -- Pensacola Historical Village volunteer

The Pensacola Historical Village is a guided walking museum in Pensacola's historic downtown district. The museum includes several buildings that date back to the early 1800s including the Dorr House, the Tivoli House, the Old Christ Church, the Lear Rocheblaue House, and the Museum of Industry. Most of the buildings are in their original locations and many of them may well be occupied...*by their original residents*.

Clara Barkley Dorr, a widow whose husband made a fortune in the booming lumber industry, built the Dorr House in 1871. For a short time, the home served as the community's schoolhouse.

The president of the University of West Florida lives in the upper floors of the home. The downstairs is open to the public as part of the Pensacola Historical Village. Over the years, guides working in the home have seen human-shaped shadows in their peripheral vision that seem to wisp about just out of their sight. Many tour guides say they *feel them* even when they can't see them.

One guide had a close encounter with the spirit of the Dorr House. The guide was standing at the top of the stairs describing the Dorr family to Village visitors. She described Mrs. Dorr as "fat" and suddenly felt a hard shove to her back that almost caused her to fall down the stairs.[9]

The guides say that objects in the home are often moved from room to room or placed "away." Guides regularly set items in the home for display as part of the tour and then move them or reset them when a group is finished in preparation for the next group. Many times when guides return to the rooms to reset the items, they find that they have already been returned to their respective places.[6]

Guides who find themselves alone in the home often feel something tugging at their pant legs or skirts as if a small child were trying to get their attention.

The Tivoli House on Village grounds was built in 1805. The building served as a house of entertainment for the rowdier of the community including those who dabbled in drinking, dancing, gambling, and the company of ladies of the evening. In 1837 an Episcopal Bishop who visited the area to dedicate the Christ Church complained that his sermon had been interrupted by the music emanating from the Tivoli House. Shortly after, a territorial ordinance prohibited such behavior in the town center.[9]

The building now serves as the Pensacola Historical Village ticket office and gift shop. A shopkeeper eating lunch in the back room one day heard someone walking around in the shop. She stepped to the front of the shop and saw a woman who seemed very out of place standing in the corner of the room. She was wearing a long, white dress that looked out of date. The shopkeeper walked toward her cautiously and asked her if she needed help with anything. The woman became visibly agitated and then... *faded* from view.

The Old Christ Church was built in 1835 as the Episcopal Church for some of the original settlers of downtown Pensacola. It is now a favored wedding venue, a popular stop for Village visitors, and an equally popular stop on the Pensacola Historical Museum's haunted walking tour.

Shortly after the church was established, three rectors died and were buried on the grounds. Over the years, the church building was expanded and was built over the rectors' graves. A recent archaeological dig uncovered them. The remains were exhumed and a funeral and reburial ceremony was held at the church.

In preparation for the event, a local carpenter was hired to build wooden caskets for the rectors' remains. He was working on the caskets alone in his shop one evening. He glanced up and saw three men standing a few feet away from him wearing long, black robes. He flinched and they were gone.[9]

During the funeral, one of the archeologists noticed three men he did not recognize walking with the church patrons. The men wore long, dark robes and scarf-like clothes around their necks. Their feet were bare. One of the men was carrying a black booklet with a cross embossed on the cover. The man looked very solemn. The other two men were laughing and talking jovially with each other.[9]

The archeologist watched the men walk with the group for several moments. When he looked away, they were gone. He later learned that it was traditional for priests of the time to be buried in their robes with a stole on their collar, barefoot, and with their prayer book. Research uncovered that the men fit the physical description of the rectors.[9]

The Lear-Rocheblave House of the Pensacola Historical Village was built in 1890 as the family home for John and Kate Lear. The home sits just across from the Tivoli House. Before the Village acquired the home, it was the private residence of an elderly gentleman who lived in the home alone. He welcomed many visitors, but kept one of the upstairs bedrooms locked at all times.[9]

A painter, who was working on a ladder on the outside of the home, glanced into the window as he was painting. He was shocked to see a *transparent* woman wearing a Victorian-style dress dancing around the room.[9]

He rushed down the ladder to tell the other workers what he had seen. They looked through every room in the house. They couldn't find the lady, nor could they find the source of the sweet, perfumery smell that permeated the home.

The dancing lady has also been seen on several occasions by people who have rented the home.[9]

Artifacts from the Old Christ Church archaeological dig were stored in the Lear-Rocheblave House during the renovations including the remains of the rectors. The rectors' remains were laid in boxes with all of their bones in order. One morning, the archaeologists returned to the home and found that the rectors' bones had been moved around in their boxes.[9]

The Museum of Industry showcases the history of Pensacola's fishing, brick making, railroad, and lumber industries in the 1800s through photographs, tools, and equipment. Many visitors to the Museum report a sense of "discomfort" especially in the back of the museum. One of the guides found herself alone in the building and was shaken when she heard a loud male voice boom at her to "Get out!"

Pensacola Victorian Bed and Breakfast

"We were in our living room right under the stairs. It sounded like the guests in the master suite were breaking dish after dish on the floor."

-- Barbee Major, Innkeeper,
Pensacola Victorian Bed and Breakfast

The Pensacola Victorian Bed & Breakfast is a well-loved and comfortable Victorian-style home in walking distance from historical downtown Pensacola. It once served as the home of Captain William Northup, who built the home in 1892 to showcase the fortune he had built in the fishing and shipping trades.

The Pensacola Victorian Bed & Breakfast is a well-loved and comfortable Victorian-style home in walking distance from historical downtown Pensacola. It once served as the home of Captain William Northup, who built the home in 1892 to showcase the fortune he had amassed in the fishing and shipping trades.

Following Northup's death in 1925, Edwin and Louise Northup and their children moved into the home. A musically gifted family, the Northup's often entertained musicians in the home, which also served as the birthplace of the Pensacola Symphony Orchestra. The home is now owned by Barbee and Chuck Major, innkeepers of the Pensacola Victorian Bed & Breakfast.[10]

The Majors and guests of the Bed & Breakfast have seen the apparition of a woman wearing a white nightgown walking around the inn and into the guest rooms. They often hear classical music from an unknown source playing throughout the home as well as the sounds of children playing and giggling and balls bouncing in the attic and in the hallways.

"A number of different guests have told us over the years that they hear what sounds like a mother cooking in a kitchen with young children playing around her feet above them in the attic," says Barbee.

"They are comforting sounds."

Barbee suspected that there was something special about the home early on. "Because of the age

Innkeepers and guests of the Pensacola Victorian Bed & Breakfast have heard footsteps and the sounds of children playing and seen movement in their peripheral vision on the main staircase that leads to the second-floor guest rooms.

of the home, I felt there might be something in the way of spirits here," she said.

"I just quietly spoke to any spirits who might be around, telling them if they were kind and peaceful they were welcome to stay, but if they weren't, then they really were not welcome."

Voices also have been heard in the dining room and the sounds of glasses and dishes being gently banged together as if someone was preparing breakfast. Often, the smells of French toast and scrambled eggs waft through the home awakening guests long before Barbee has begun preparing the guests' breakfast.

One evening the Majors heard dishes breaking one after another upstairs in the master suite. In the morning, the guests staying in the master suite asked Barbee why she was breaking dishes in the kitchen. Barbee often hears guests walking about the rooms and the stairs when there are no registered guests in the inn.

The Majors say that they have never felt threatened by anything in their home. Although…previous innkeepers have had a different experience. One former innkeeper of the home had completed decorating all of the upstairs bedrooms and was walking around the rooms enjoying her work. When she stepped into the room that was Captain Northup's bedroom, she was pushed to the wall by an unseen force. A man's voice whispered in her ear, "This is your house now. Look after it." Guests staying in the Captain's room regularly smell the scent of pipe tobacco.

A playwright who was visiting Pensacola to work with a local theatre came home late in the evening from dinner and saw a woman in long Victorian-style nightdress with brown hair walking into one of the

Innkeepers and guests of the Pensacola Victorian Bed & Breakfast have seen the apparition of a woman in a long, white nightgown walking into the room directly across from the Bed and Breakfast's front staircase.

rooms that had been vacated that morning. He thought, 'How great that Barbee rented the room again.' The next morning, however, he learned that the room had not been rented and there was no one staying at the Bed & Breakfast that matched her description.

"His eyes grew incredibly wide when I told him no one was staying in that room," said Barbee.

Chuck may also have seen this spirit. He was standing in the foyer at the bottom of the main staircase and saw a woman enter the master suite that he thought was Barbee.

"Later on he asked if it was me," says Barbee, "but I had been on the other side of the house in our living quarters and nowhere near the master suite. There was also no one staying at the Bed & Breakfast on this particular night."

Heather, another guest of the inn, was sitting on the couch in the front room at 6 a.m. enjoying a cup of coffee. She watched shadows move around on the landing at the top of the main staircase. It looked like the uninhibited movements of an impatient child. She kept waiting to see the child and its parent walk down the stairs.

"I thought it was another guest coming down for coffee, but no one ever did," Heather said. "I noticed later that when I walked on the landing it made a lot of noise. There was no noise with the movement I saw."

Reverend Jamie Sanders, who often performs wedding ceremonies in the Bed & Breakfast, says he knew the first time he stepped foot in the home that there was something special about it.

"The moment I reached the top of the stairs I felt something," says Jamie.

On another occasion, Jamie was on the grounds of the Bed & Breakfast blessing its new Café. He noticed a shadowy figure in the shape of a man standing in a window of the master suite. He looked away for a moment and the image was gone.

"I love it here," says Barbee. "I don't mind that they are here. I think they love it here too."

Monticello

The town of Monticello is a small community about twenty-five miles from Tallahassee. In 1818, it was the last of the area surrounded by Tallahassee to be mostly inhabited by Native Americans. In the 1820s settlers discovered the area and began establishing cotton plantations and large stately homes. The area grew quickly because of its proximity to the state capital. Soon, the town was coined Monticello and its surrounding land Jefferson County after the United States Capital.

The Monticello Opera House

The Monticello Opera House sits within the Perkins Block, a large brick building in historic Monticello built in 1890 by John H. Perkins. The building stands out in the small historic town, sitting proudly on Washington Street just to the left of the of the town hall. Perkins Block is a treasured piece of Monticello's history and the most well-known building for its haunted folklore.

The Monticello Opera House sits within the Perkins Block, a large brick building in historic Monticello built in 1890 by John H. Perkins. The building stands out in the small historic town, sitting proudly on Washington Street, just to the left of the town hall. In its day, the Perkins Block included general, sewing, hardware, and farm supply stores and famously, its Opera House.

For many years in the late 1800s, the wealthy Northerners wintering in Monticello and the surrounding areas traveled to the theatre by horse and buggy. Stables behind the Perkins Block sold horses, mules, and wagons. The wealthy patrons entered the theatre through the large stained-glass doors in the front of the building and sat on the main floor of the theatre. Their drivers were welcome to view the show from the balcony seating above.[11]

In the early 1900s the railroads that provided easy access to Monticello were re-routed. The once bustling little town was by-passed and wealthy patrons who visited with such regularity began spending their winters elsewhere. Live performances were discontinued.[11]

After an unsuccessful attempt to use the Block as a movie theatre, the auditorium was locked indefinitely and its stained-glass windows were boarded. The Block's shops still served the local community.[11]

In 1972, the Monticello Opera Company was formed with the goal of providing opportunities for young performers. The group raised funds and revived the Opera House. The theatre was carefully restored and still features much of its original décor including antique moldings, decorative woodwork, high-reaching stained glass windows, and its original creaky hardwood floors. The Perkins Block once again houses the Opera House. The Block's large rooms are also rented for private parties and weddings. Today the Perkins Block is a treasured piece of town history and the most well-known building of Monticello's haunted folklore.[11]

Jan Rickey, who has been managing the Perkins Block for twenty years, says visitors to the Opera House feel especially strange in the theatre. And those who spend any amount of time in the theatre never feel alone.

Photos taken in the Opera House often feature many round orb-like objects.

"The Perkins Block is visited frequently by town residents and tourists," says Jan. "Most visitors comment that they just feel strange in the theatre.

"A lot of people sense a presence as soon as they walk in there. It's not at all unusual for people who don't know about the building's folklore and who don't believe in ghosts to walk into the theatre and say, 'Wow, there is something special here.'"

Jan believes the feeling that so many people experience in the building may be the ghost of Mr. Perkins who had a strong affection for the theatre. She also says it may be the spirit of a man who was badly burned in the 1900s while lighting the gaslights in the basement. He died from his injuries.

Locals say that the spirits of the Perkins Block may not all be Opera House related. According to town legend, the Block sits on the location of a grisly murder. Legend has it that a bakery owned by two brothers once stood on that spot. One evening the brothers began to argue over a woman. They became enraged, and one brother killed the other and then burned down the bakery.

Residents also point to the large tree that sits next to the Block as a likely reason visitors feel a presence there. The tree served as the town meeting spot for Civil War troops. Soldiers would gather

Classical music is often heard emanating from the auditorium piano of the Opera House when no one is in the auditorium.

A tree just outside of the Perkins Block served as the town meeting spot for Civil War troops reporting for battle. The tree also served as the town "hanging tree" for those who went astray of the law.

there before leaving for battle. The tree also served as the town "hanging tree" for those who went astray of the law.

Visitors and caretakers of the Block often hear indiscernible voices in the building's hallways and large empty rooms. They hear footsteps on the wood floors when they know they are alone in the building. They often have the sensation that someone is standing closely behind them.

"You have that feeling like someone is so close to you that they are going to breathe on your neck," says Jan. "You turn around and there's no one there. But you can still feel their presence."

At least once a year the piano in the theatre is heard playing something classical when there is no one but Jan in the building. She can hear the music through the ceiling in her office. When she walks toward the stairs to investigate, the music stops.

"It always stops at the same time," says Jan. "It stops when I reach the auditorium stairs."

Jan says the biggest challenge at the Block is keeping track of the keys. Because the Block's rooms are used for parties, many of the cabinets that house dining ware and other materials for catering are locked in different cabinets. Although staff members store the cabinet keys in the same place in the kitchen, they always seem to be missing when someone needs them. Jan says the trick is to not look for them.

"The keys to the cabinets disappear and then re-appear moments later where they were left," Jan says. "It's happened so many times we expect it.

"We just leave the room and come back a few minutes later and there they are right where we left them."

Several visitors to the Block have witnessed full-body apparitions in the building. One year during the Jefferson County High School prom two teachers became very upset when they saw a "dark shadowy man" moving around among the students.

Photos taken in the Block's theatre almost always capture odd glowing orb-shaped objects that seem to move about the main seating area, the balcony, and the stage.

"You become used to it," says Jan. "It's always felt benign to me. But anyone who works here for any amount of time knows they are never alone."

The John Denham House

The John Denham House of Monticello sits in a quiet corner of a quaint town much as it did when a Scottish immigrant constructed it in the early 1870s. The home welcomes guests with its large front porch and Greek revival architecture.[9]

The John Denham house was constructed for William Denham, a merchant and county judge, who moved to Monticello from Dunbar, Scotland, with two sisters and three brothers. Later, it was the home of William Denham's son James, who served as the mayor of Monticello and as a representative in the Florida House of Representatives.[12]

The house is now operated as a Bed and Breakfast by innkeeper Pat Inman. Guests of the John Denham House seem welcomed not only by the charm of Monticello – one of the oldest settlements in the Panhandle – but also by something or someone else.

Electronic devices such as cameras and cell phones do not hold a charge in the home especially on the second floor where the guest rooms are located. Many guests have purchased new batteries for cameras and other devices only to have them drain shortly after returning to their room. Batteries drain almost immediately in the home's cupola.

"You have to move pretty quickly to take a photo from the Cupola," says Pat.

Batteries are not the only electrical devices that exhibit strange behavior in the Denham House. Several times a month all of the

The John Denham House of Monticello sits on a quiet corner of a quaint town much as it did when it was constructed by a Scottish immigrant in the early 1870s. The home welcomes guests with its large front porch and Greek revival architecture. Electronic devices such as cameras and cell phones do not hold a charge in the home.

Camera and flashlight batteries drain almost immediately in the home's cupola and the staircase that leads to it.

In the guest rooms of the John Denham House, guests report eerie feelings, unpredictable clock alarms, and lights that seem turn on and off by themselves.

five guest-room alarm clocks sound off at the same time in the middle of the day.

"It's completely random," says Pat. "The alarm of every clock in the house will go off around 2:30 or 3 in the afternoon."

Guest room lights seem to turn on and off by themselves even when guests are in their rooms. Many guests of the John Denham House comment that they don't feel "alone" when they are in their rooms or anywhere else in the home.

According to Pat, the "Blue Room" is the strangest room in the home. Women of childbearing age who stay in that room often are awakened in the middle of the night by all of the lights in the room suddenly turning on.

"I warn them now," says Pat, "or put them in a different room. Most guests think it's funny."

In the upstairs hallway of the John Denham House, a guest reported seeing a man in what she described as "period dress" standing in the large hallway that connects the upstairs guest rooms.

Several guests of the John Denham House have reported seeing apparitions. One guest reported seeing a man in what she described as "period dress" standing in the large upstairs hallway that connects all of the guest rooms. Another guest was awakened in the middle of the night by a man standing at the foot of her bed.

Although Pat happily welcomes all people to enjoy the hospitality of the John Denham House, almost all male gay couples who have stayed at the inn have left in the middle of the night saying little if anything more than, "We just can't stay here."

"It's a weird situation for me," says Jan. "I welcome gay guests at the Inn. Many couples have stayed here. I've never had a female couple leave the inn that way. No matter how many times I ask them what happened and plead with them to stay, they leave in a hurry and without an explanation."

The Palmer House

The Palmer House of Monticello is a piece of town folklore. It is the former residence of Dr. John Dabney Palmer.

The Palmer House of Monticello is a piece of town folklore. The simple, white, unassuming home that sits just outside of the town's center courthouse was the former residence of Dr. John Dabney Palmer. Dr. Palmer studied and experimented with pharmaceuticals in the small building just outside of the main house. It was in that small office that he developed a brand of cough medicine he patented "666."[13]

In 1880, the house was sold to John H. Perkins, a prominent businessman. In 1890, he built the Perkins Block that sits just up the road from the home.[13]

The Palmer House was also owned by Richard and Dorothy Simpson. The couple had no children. Dorothy ran an antique shop out of the home, but locals say it was rare when she would agree to part with any of the items on display. When Dorothy died, the home was left to her estate.

Owners of the Palmer House of Monticello have heard footsteps walking and running down the stairs when they are alone in the home. The homeowners' great grandson saw the apparition of a "blue man" standing at the foot of the stairs.

The Palmer House has changed ownership many times over the years. Locals claim that no one owns it for long because the house has a feeling to it that makes some feel drawn to it and others uncomfortable.

Owners and visitors of the home hear the sounds of someone walking as well as running down the stairs. They hear disembodied female voices and have felt extremely cold air being blown into their ears.

Jackie Anders, the home's current owner, felt drawn to the property.

"I always wanted this house," she says. "I would drive by it all of the time and just look at it."

When the house became available, Jackie's husband purchased the home as a gift for her birthday and, he hoped, a place for her to sell some of the many antiques and collectables she had gathered over the years. The couple began packing up the items that remained in the home and planning for its restoration. That's when Jackie, who was alone in the house, first realized that there was *something odd* about the Palmer House....

It was a hot July night. Jackie was working in the home alone at about 12 a.m. She was in the parlor packing items in boxes. Suddenly, a wave of frigid air blew into her face and then whipped around her body. The frigid air hung around her for several minutes before fading away.

"It was so hot I thought I was going to die. I was just packing up everything just as busy as I could be," says Jackie. "It scared me so bad. I said, 'Dorothy, if this is you bothering me, let me know because I'll sit down and talk with you. I'm not afraid to do that, but don't scare me.'"

Owners of the Palmer House have experienced the sensation of frigid air being blown in their ears in the home's pink room.

Jackie's daughter, JoAnne, had a similar experience. JoAnne was work-

Owners of the Palmer House have heard the sounds of a female voice babbling incoherently in one of the downstairs bedrooms.

Dr. John Dabney Palmer, namesake of the Palmer House, studied and experimented with pharmaceuticals in the small cottage outside of the main house. It was in that small office that he developed a brand of cough medicine he called "666."

ing upstairs in the home's "pink room." Suddenly a burst of frigid air blew directly into her ear.

"She screamed, 'Mama!', and cupped her ear," says Jackie. "She didn't pack up upstairs after that."

Throughout the renovations, Jackie and others working in the home regularly heard footsteps walking and running down the stairs when there was no one else in the home. A tape player that Jackie had in the home during the renovations would turn on seemingly by itself, blaring music throughout the house, and then turn off.

One night Jackie was alone in the home sitting on a wicker bench in the pink room upstairs, quietly enjoying the fruits of the day's labor. She heard very loud footsteps walk from the nearby bedroom across the hallway to the doorway of the pink room and then stop. She called, "What is it that you want?" The noise stopped.

An elderly man who had grown up in the Palmer House visited Jackie shortly after she acquired the home. He told her that the pink room was his childhood bedroom and asked her if she knew that her house was "haunted." He said almost every night that he spent in the home, he was visited by something.

One of the strangest occurrences in the Palmer House was experienced by Jackie's great grandson, Colby. He was two and a half at the time. He was staying at the home with Jackie while his mother attended college.

Colby was enjoying himself, running from the hallway and the back parlor to the front door, but became very frightened when he saw a man standing at the bottom of the stairs with purple-tinted skin wearing a black suit. "His little heart was racing so fast," says Jackie. "I took him in my arms. He was trembling."

Jackie carried him to the front of the house and showed him that the door was locked and that no one was there.

On another occasion, Jackie was meeting with an antique dealer in the home. They were standing in the hallway when they both heard a female voice babbling incoherantly. He turned to Jackie and said, "I thought we were alone." They followed the voice to a corner of one of the bedrooms.

"Things have calmed down since the renovations were completed," says Jackie, "but I can still hear them walking up and down the stairs and into the rooms. The first thing I do when I walk in here is say, 'good morning everybody.'"

The Daffodale House

"There are creatures that roam around in the country at night. I am familiar with them. This was different. There was something about it that just wasn't right.

"When I imagine scary, when I imagine evil... that noise is what I imagine."

-- Scott Ebberbach,
Daffodale Homeowner

The Daffodale House of Monticello is a meandering Victorian mansion situated among pine and oak trees a short distance from the Monticello town center. Owners of the mansion have heard disembodied growling in the kitchen and seen the apparition of a woman floating in an upstairs bedroom.

The Daffodale house is a meandering Victorian mansion situated among pine and oak trees a short distance from the Monticello town center. The home was built from

Homeowners of the Daffodale House captured this image of a ghostly figure moving down a back hallway of the mansion.

1897 to 1904 as a showpiece for a wealthy banker who wanted to build a home that mirrored the structural integrity of a bank building. His ancestors, many of whom still live in Monticello, describe him as a man of great power and wealth. Builders who have looked at the home's structure have commented that it was built "several times over."

Scott and Cathy Ebberbach purchased the home in 2006 as a renovation project. They envisioned the home and its extensive grounds as an upscale Bed and Breakfast and restaurant as well as a venue for weddings and parties. As the couple began renovating the home, they realized there was a little bit more to the Daffodale House than they expected. One-by-one... *strange occurrences began happening in the home and on its grounds*.

A gardener the Ebberbachs hired to clean up the many Camellia trees on the Daffodale property ran screaming from the grounds and refused to return to work. When Scott was finally able to get her to talk about why she was leaving, she told him there was an apparition of an African American man in the trees.

The gardener was pulling broken branches from a patch of Camellia trees. She noticed a rustling in the trees directly in front of her and looked up. A dark-skinned man was rising from the trees. She stood frozen as his head, then his shoulders, and the rest of his body *materialized* in front of her. She threw her gloves and rake and took off running.

It wasn't long before the Ebberbachs began having experiences of their own. The family hears footsteps on the hardwood floors of the fourth floor attic that was once living quarters, but is now used for storage. All three locks on the front door unlock

Homeowners of the Daffodale House often hear footsteps in the attic directly above their bedroom.

seemingly by themselves almost every night. It is a heavy, Dutch-style door cut large enough to accommodate a coffin.

"I go downstairs every night and pinch myself to make sure I'm not dreaming. I lock all three locks and the next morning...all three of the locks are unlocked," says Scott.

"The footsteps on the fourth floor have become more and more eerie for me," Scott continues. "In an old house the structure makes noise. You get to know the noises in an old house. But there are times when you hear ... things you cannot explain on the wood floors especially on the third floor.

"There is definitely something on the top of this house that hangs out here. It walks all over the floors up there."

The Ebberbachs also have learned that if they leave the home for any length of time, its best to remove the light bulbs from the fixtures in the front rooms. Several times they have turned all of the lights off in the home and locked up for a weekend trip. When night falls, the next door neighbor calls to let them know that the downstairs lights are on.

"It never happens when we are in the house," says Scott, "but any night we are not here, those lights turn on."

Scott and Cathy often see movement in their peripheral vision. They also often hear a female voice whisper their name into their ears.

"It's when you are looking at something else that you see them," says Scott.

During renovations, Scott and one of the Ebberbachs' sons were laying tile on a back hallway floor. As they laid the last tile, Scott took a picture of their work. The picture captured a glowing human figure moving through the hallway.

Shortly after that, a man came to the door and introduced himself as an exorcist. He asked how the family had acquired the home, how they were doing, and if they were having any problems with which he might be able to assist.

The exorcist explained that he had been hired by a previous owner to extricate an "evil entity" that was plaguing the family. He commented, *"There is something under your house that might give you some problems."*

The Ebberbachs did not purchase his services, choosing to have a more positive attitude about the activity in their home. They don't deny that there seems to be strange benevolent activity in their home. At times they do experience something else ... *SOMETHING* Scott describes as feeling *evil*.

"There has obviously been something here for a

Homeowners of the Daffodale House have seen the apparition of a woman wearing a flowing, white gown in front of the fireplace in the Safari Room.

long time," says Scott. "It was enough for former residents to hire an exorcist. And I do agree...there is something that feels evil here.

"But it's not all evil. I don't have any problem with them being here."

One of the few things that actually scared the Ebberbachs was a series of phone calls that have since stopped. The phone would ring. The Ebberbachs would answer and hear a low, far-off, female voice mumbling something indiscernible with empty air in the background. Many times they would come home to find messages with these sounds on their answering machine.

"Those were scary," says Scott. "My wife is not easily scared, but they really gave her the 'heeby jeebies.'"

A former resident of the Daffodale House who lived in one of the attic rooms said his personal items were often picked up and tossed around the room by unseen hands. His television turned on and off by itself and changed channels. He would unplug it when he left his room and find it plugged in and playing when he returned.

One night Scott was alone in the home. He was having trouble sleeping and decided to take his stereo and speakers up to the master bedroom and listen to Earth, Wind & Fire to drown out his uneasiness. He lay on his bed, turned up the volume as loud as he could stand it, and closed his eyes.

Suddenly, he heard a pounding noise on the ceiling above his head. He lay there, listening to it pound over and over again for several moments before he could gather the courage to roll over and turn down the volume.

"I couldn't believe it. It sounded like someone was hitting the wood floor of the attic with a sledgehammer," says Scott. He acquainted the noise with a childhood experience.

"When I was a kid, I lived on the sixth floor of an apartment building in the Bronx (New York). There was a man who lived on the fifth floor. He was not a well man. He would pound on the floor when we angered him. I know what that sounds like.

"I had an overwhelming feeling that I needed to stop the music, but I couldn't move.

"I didn't like that feeling. And I wouldn't want to do that again."

An antique elevator that once took homeowners between the first and second floors of the home still sits just outside of the master bedroom. Although the homeowners and guests do not smoke in the house, there is an ever-present smell of pipe smoke in the hallway near the elevator. Locals say that in the 1900s the homeowners' nanny regularly smoked a pipe in that hallway just outside of the children's bedrooms.

The "safari room," as homeowners call it for its namesake safari-themed decorations, is another area of the home where its residents have encountered the unexpected.

One of the Ebberbachs' sons was staying in the room. He was having trouble sleeping. At 3 a.m., he looked to the room's fireplace and saw a woman wearing a sheer, white nightgown hovering above the floor. She was facing the doorway. Her mouth was moving as if she was speaking, but there was no sound.

"He ran into our room like a maniac," says Scott. "I saw genuine fear in my son."

On another occasion, Scott was alone in the home for a weekend. He decided to enjoy his solitude by walking around the house in the nude. As he was descending the main staircase, he heard shrieks of adult, female laughter that sounded so close to him that he turned around to see if someone else was on the stairs. He scrambled for his robe and looked out the windows, but he couldn't find the source of the laughter.

"I was kind of offended," says Scott. "I was nude and they were laughing at my body. It was not a giggle. It was more like a belly laugh. I don't do that anymore."

Although the Ebberbachs have become accustomed to the strange activity throughout the Daffodale House, no member of the household spends any length of time in the kitchen that is not required.

The small kitchen sits in back of the home. It is full of light that streams in from several windows and a back door. Yet, it is consistently thirty degrees colder than the rest of the house even in the worst heat of the summer. The Ebberbachs and many visitors to the home comment that there is an "uninviting feeling" in that room. Most visitors don't stay in the room for long and Scott admits the family's behavior mimics that of their guests.

"We don't hang around in that room. It's not a comfortable room," he says.

For Scott, it's not just a feeling. One day he entered the kitchen from the back door. As he was walking past the oven, the room became frigidly cold. He hesitated and then heard a low, deep growl that sounded as if it were coming from a large animal inches away from him.

"I was frozen. The hair was standing up on the back of my neck. It was the kind of growl an animal makes right before it pounces.

"My first thought was 'I need to make it to the dining room door.'"

"There are creatures that roam around in the country at night," says Scott. "I am familiar with them. This was different. There was something about it that just wasn't right.

"When I imagine scary, when I imagine evil...*THAT noise is what I imagine.*"

The Ebberbachs have come to accept that their house is different. Although the home is currently for sale, they still embrace their home's haunted reputation, offering private ghost tours to visitors and even dressing up in costume to participate in the Big Bend Ghost Trackers Historic Monticello Ghost Tours. During several haunted tours, visitors have witnessed the curtains in the upstairs bedrooms flailing wildly about in the windows by themselves.

"I try to look at the entities here as good," says Scott. "They may not even know they are dead. They may be doing the same thing they'll be doing for eternity whether this house is here or not.

"I know now that they are here. It's not odd that they are here. It's just God's plan. No one can tell me that we don't have a soul."

5

Tallahassee

In the 1500s the land that is now Tallahassee was home to the Apalachee Native Americans. An expedition led by Spanish explorer Panfilo de Narvaez in 1528 is thought to be the first time Europeans arrived in the area. Many other expeditions followed. In 1633, Spain established Fort San Luis, a mission chain from St. Augustine to Tallahassee.

In 1704 Creek Native Americans and British forces destroyed the missions. These Native Americans and others in the area became known by settlers as Seminoles. In 1763, Spain offered England ownership of the area of Tallahassee in exchange for Cuba. In 1783 Spain regained possession of the area. In 1818 General Andrew Jackson successfully invaded Florida and in 1821 becomes Governor of Florida.

In 1824, the Territorial Legislature of Florida named Tallahassee the state Capital. Settlers came to the area in droves as plans were developed for churches, stores, and home sites and the city's population quickly more than tripled.[14, 16]

Goodwood Museum and Gardens

> *"We saw things moving out of the corners of our eyes and in the reflection of the mirrors. When it got really cold, we tried not to look."*
>
> -- Liane Schrader, former intern,
> Goodwood Museum and Gardens

The Goodwood Museum and Gardens of Tallahassee is a popular attraction for tourists passing through Tallahassee, as well as year-round residents. Interns report feeling cold spots throughout the house and seeing movement in their peripheral vision.

The Goodwood Museum and Gardens is a popular attraction for tourists passing through Tallahassee as well as year-round residents. Its rich history and sprawling sixteen acres of carefully manicured lawn lined with centuries-old oak trees inspire many to explore the Museum, attend Goodwood's

Volunteers and interns have seen movement reflected in the mirrors and in the home's crystal chandeliers.

numerous cultural events held throughout the year, and even hold weddings on its meandering grounds.

Goodwood was built in the 1830s as a full-time home for North Carolina native, Hardy Croom, and his wife and three children, but the Crooms never got a chance to live in their Tallahassee home. The steamship they were traveling on sank in the waters of the Atlantic and the entire family drowned.

Hardy's brother, Bryan, took ownership of the home, but soon lost it to Hardy Croom's sister-in-law in a lawsuit that was fought until 1857. Later Arva Hopkins and her husband purchased the home.[15]

The Hopkins loved to entertain. Goodwood became a hotspot for Tallahassee's social elite during the 1880s. In 1885, Arva sold the estate to an Englishman named William Lamb Arrowsmith and his wife Elizabeth. William died within months of moving into the home. Elizabeth remained at Goodwood for twenty-five years. In 1911, she sold the home and its grounds to a wealthy widow by the name of Mrs. Alexander Tiers.[15]

Volunteers learn quickly not to stand with their backs to the dining room fireplace. In addition to it being a perfect angle to see the activity in all three of the room's mirrors, volunteers commented that in that spot it feels as though someone is standing behind you so close that if you moved even an inch you might bump them.

In 1925, Senator William Hodges' wife, Margaret, fell in love with one of the beds at Goodwood. When the Senator could not work out a deal to purchase the bed, he purchased the home and all of its furnishings to obtain it for her.[15]

The two lived in the home together until William's death in 1940. Margaret remained in the home and rented out several guest cottages that were on the grounds. In 1948, she married Tomas Hood, an Army officer who had been renting one of the cottages. In 1978, Margaret died and Tom established the Margaret E. Wilson Foundation that manages the Goodwood Museum and Gardens.[15]

The house and the grounds of the museum and gardens are well-known in Tallahassee and surrounding cities as a special place — timeless, beautiful, and romantic. But those who have spent a great deal of time in the home, especially the dining room, have experienced other sensations there. Volunteers feel sharp cold spots that seem to move from room to room, and some volunteers have described the second level of the home as "heavy."

Volunteers learn quickly not to stand with their backs to the dining room fireplace. In addition to it being a perfect angle to see the unexplained movement in all three of the room's mirrors, volunteers say that in that spot it feels as though someone is standing behind you so close that if you move even an inch you might bump them.

One intern who was left alone in the home became so agitated that she quickly exited through the nearest door and waited on the front porch for someone to return before going back to resume her work.

Interns say the activity in the home was especially disturbing during the cataloging of artifacts that took place shortly after the home was bequeathed to the state of Florida.

Volunteers, staff, and interns were charged with cataloging every item in the home. Piece by piece they placed items on the dining room table, marked them with a number, and recorded them on the home's office record. Workers soon realized that some items were more likely to cause activity than others.

"Some days everything seemed normal," says Liane Schrader, a former Goodwood intern. "Other days, like the day we worked on the china cabinet contents, were very strange.

"You would pick up a particular item and the room would become extremely cold and so quiet, you could here yourself breathe."

"It wasn't that you felt threatened there, but you always had the sensation that you were in someone else's house and that they thought you shouldn't be there."

The Knott House

"I heard footsteps — someone walking upstairs on the wood floors and I thought, 'It's Lucy,' and then I remembered, she had gone home hours ago."'
-- Former Knott House Museum manager

The Knott House Museum of Tallahassee is believed to have been built in 1843 by a free African American man named George Proctor. Museum staff often hear footsteps on the floors above their offices when they are alone in the home. *Courtesy of the Knott House Museum, a site of the Museum of Florida History.*

I n historical downtown Tallahassee, small canopy-tree shaded roads wind around antique southern homes and towering new construction bringing the worlds of the 1800s and the new millennium together in an odd mix of old southern architecture and burgeoning modern business.

A photo taken in the study of the Knott House Museum during the restoration process captured what former staff members believe to be the ghost of Charlie Knott. *Courtesy of the Knott House Museum, a site of the Museum of Florida History.*

In the heart of this mix sits one of Tallahassee's most quiet hauntings, the Knott House Museum. The Museum and former home of the Knott family is located at the corner of East Park Avenue and Calhoun Street. It is a welcoming place with a large front porch situated just steps from the sidewalk of Park Avenue. The home is an integral part of the folklore of Tallahassee, a well-known haunting among locals who believe the spirit of Charlie Knott, its final resident, has yet to depart.

The Knott House is believed to have been built in 1843 by a free African American man by the name of George Proctor. The home was a wedding gift from attorney Thomas Hagner to his wife Catherine Gamble. Thomas died in the Knott House two short years later. Catherine, devastated by her loss, never remarried.

She opened Knott House for boarders and remained there for nine years, raising the couples' two children. In 1857, she left the home and moved in with her widowed mother and aunt.[17]

In 1865, the Civil War ended with the surrender of Robert E. Lee. News of the surrender and what it meant to the South's slaves took one week to reach Tallahassee. On May 10 of that year, Union troops occupied the city. Federal troops spread throughout the town announcing freedom to area slaves. Brigadier General Edward McCook commandeered the Knott House and read the Emancipation Proclamation from its porch.[17]

In 1883, Catherine Gamble Hagner sold the Knott House to Dr. George Betton, who ran a medical practice out of the home's basement. Dr. Betton apprenticed former slave and carriage driver William J. Gunn in the practice of medicine and paid for him to study medicine in Tennessee. In 1882, Dr. Gunn became Florida's first African American physician, treating patients from his office on Tallahassee's Duval Street. Dr. Betton passed away in the Knott House in 1896.[17]

In 1919, Dr. John W. and Caroline Scott purchased the Knott House. The recently retired Dr. Scott became bedridden within a year of purchasing the home. He died in the Knott House in 1920.[17]

William and Luella Knott purchased the home in 1928. William was the state treasurer. Luella was a very social woman with a gift for writing poetry and an interest in alternative medicine. William and Luella lived in the Knott House happily for almost thirty-seven years. Their three children, Mary Frank, Charlie, and James, also lived in the home.[17]

As William attended to the needs of a state recovering from the Great Depression as Florida's first state auditor and then as comptroller and treasurer, Luella championed her own causes. She lobbied successfully to ban the sale of alcohol in the area and was involved in many charities.[17] A talented poet, Luella often decorated her home with whimsical poetry hand-written on pieces of paper.

Luella was also obsessed with her health and the health of her family. Orphaned at the age of eight by tuberculosis, Luella was acutely attuned to her body. She believed in taking long periods of rest and often traveled to the offices of Dr. John Kellogg of Michigan, the founder of Kellogg's Corn Flakes; he was a physician whose practices of vegetarianism, exercise, and the flushing of toxins were considered questionable by the standards of that time.

After a long, happy life, William died in the Knott House in 1965 at the age of 101. Luella followed just eight days later. As with every occasion in her life, Luella penned her final poem just before her death, stating that perhaps her William was calling her from beyond:

> "...The light grows dimmer every day...
> Sweet sorrows taught me how to see...
> And hear and feel ... and want to be....
> With that dear voice that's calling me..."[18]

Charlie Knott, a life-long bachelor, continued to live in the Knott House. He closed the living, dining, and study rooms and left them as a shrine to his parents. He died in the home in 1985.

The official stance from the Florida Department of State, which manages archiving and preservation, is that the Knott House is *not* haunted. However, just a few years ago, when the home was managed by the Historic Tallahassee Preservation Board, many ghost tours were held in the home that included the viewing of a photograph taken in the home's library during its renovation that clearly shows the apparition of a man sitting in front of a bookcase.

Visitors to the Knott House frequently experience cold spots. Staff members and volunteers say that along with the cold, there is a difficult to describe feeling that "they [Knott family members] are here." Staff has also heard the sounds of footsteps on the wooden floors of the second floor when they know no one is upstairs.

Charlie Knott was the last member of the Knott family to live in the Knott House. Charlie kept the living, dining, and study rooms as a shrine to his parents.
Courtesy of the Knott House Museum, a site of the Museum of Florida History.

One staff member recalls, "I was sitting in the office finishing up some paperwork when I kept hearing movement and footsteps above my head. It sounded as if someone was walking on the wood floors up and down the stairs and in and out of the rooms. I thought, 'it must be Lucy' and then I remembered she had gone home for the day."

Former Knott House Director Joan Matey often promoted the Museum through a program called "Fear Knott." The program explored the home's unique energy by inviting spiritually sensitive people to the home as well as those interested in the history of paranormal activity in the Knott House.

Matey commented, "In a house that has had so much life lived in it for so long, there is going to be energy left behind.

"There is definitely energy in the Knott House."

During Matey's directorship, many visitors to the home had unique experiences. During Fear Knott events, Matey sometimes invited well-known "sensitive" people to the home to discuss the home's unique energy and share the staff's experiences with visitors.

During one of these events, a guest reported "feeling" that there was a young boy in the house who was too ill to walk up the stairs. Staff research following the event revealed that early in the home's history a family with a young boy suffering from Polio had lived in the Knott House for a very short period of time.

During another Fear Knott event, a guest became overwhelmed by a vision of a large group of women collected in the living room and dressed in antebellum apparel. The vision came to her as a reflection through the large living room mirrors. The women, who were wearing hoop skirts, seemed to be looking at her through the mirror.

Staff consulted the living members of the Knott family, who explained that Luella often held social get-togethers for wealthy women in the home. At least one of which required the ladies to dress in antebellum attire and gather in the home's living room for refreshments in front of the room's large mirror.

Another Knott House visitor came for a tour at the request of his girlfriend who was volunteering at the Museum. The staff member led the couple on the standard tour of the home.

A guest to the Knott House Museum became overwhelmed by a vision of a large group of women collected in the living room dressed in antebellum apparel. The vision came to her as a reflection through the large living room mirrors.
Courtesy of the Knott House Museum, a site of the Museum of Florida History.

During the tour, the man became visibly agitated and uncomfortable. As they reached the library where the photo of the apparition had been taken, the man became very weak and fell to his knees. Every hair on his arms and legs stood straight up. He regained himself as his girlfriend and the tour guide came to his aid, but then doubled over in discomfort and left the room. He told them that although he does not admit it openly, he has in the past had a sensitivity that he cannot explain, saying, "I never wanted this...my father was this way. I hate this."

After composing himself, he returned to the library. He walked carefully and slowly to the bookcase where the photo had been taken and said, "This is where the energy is coming from." He was not aware of the photo at the time. Staff showed him the photo when the tour was complete. He left the Knott House and never returned.

The Former Sunland Hospital

The Sunland Hospital or "Sunnyland" building of Tallahassee, as some mistakenly call it, once served the community as a state-of-the-art tuberculosis hospital. Before its demolition, neighbors often heard disembodied screams emanating from the building.

In 2006, luxury apartments were built just off of Blairstone Road in Tallahassee. They are a convenient and comfortable housing solution for professionals working in Tallahassee's growing association community, colleges, and businesses. They were also built on the site of one of the most infamously haunted buildings in Florida. Until demolition and construction of the apartments began, the remains of the Sunland Sanitarium stood as a constant reminder to those traveling on Blairstone Road that wicked things happen even in places built to heal.

The Sunland Hospital, or "Sunnyland" building as some mistakenly call it, was constructed as a state-of-the-art tuberculosis hospital. In 1952, the W. T. Edwards Hospital, named for the chairman of the hospital board, opened its doors to serve those members of the community and surrounding areas who were stricken with tuberculosis. It was one of four in Florida and all of them had waiting lists of ailing patients. The hospital was a self-contained community in the country. Many doctors and nurses lived on the hospital campus.

Tuberculosis victims suffered from bacterial infections that attacked their lungs, kidney, spine, and brain. The airborne disease that caused violent coughing fits, fever, and fatigue was once the leading cause of death in the United States. The most common treatment in the 1950s was what patients referred to as "taking the cure," which meant patients would have air pumped into their lungs to speed the healing of lesions.[19]

The hospital was equipped to provide this sought-after treatment to four hundred patients at a time; as a result, many of them survived. For those who did not, the last stop in the W. T. Edwards Hospital was the morgue that was located in the basement.

Those who worked at the hospital in the 1950s say it was a nice place where patients were well cared for and staff members were friendly. In the early 1960s advancements in antibiotics were effectively treating tuberculosis victims and the number of patients were declining. The W. T. Edwards Hospital closed its doors, and the building remained vacant for several years.[19]

In 1967, the building reopened as one of six Sunland Hospitals for children afflicted with the condition then referred to as "mental retardation." The Tallahassee site was one of two that also cared

This image was taken on the second floor of the Sunland Hospital building shortly after a visitor experienced the sensation that something had moved quickly in front of her face. Note that the walls on the left side of the room and the ceiling are not blurry. The photo seems to have captured movement from the hall door to the camera.

for children with physical disabilities. It was a hospital-style facility that housed young patients in multi-bed wards. The hospital organized its patient wards by floors with those diagnosed to be the most disturbed on the lower floors.[19]

Former staff say Sunland was a fearsome place for many in the community. Prospective staff often declined employment because they found the patients' conditions disturbing.[19]

In the late 1970s, rumors began to surface that conditions at Sunland Hospital were declining. Charges were filed against the hospital for overcrowding, poor sanitation practices, poorly trained employees, and patient abuse. Hospital administrators were accused of mismanaging $13,000 of funds in patients' spending accounts and at least one employee was convicted of stealing $3,000.[19]

In addition to these charges, the hospital walls were found to be full of asbestos and coated in lead paint. In 1979, the Florida Legislature ordered both the Tallahassee and Orlando Sunland hospitals to close. Patients were dispersed to area group homes—a process that took four long years.[19]

Until the recent demolition, the Sunland building was left to crumble into disrepair. During this time many curious visitors slipped through the chain-link fence and entered the building through an opening on the basement floor to explore the remains of the building and experience the rumors of paranormal activity.

Visitors to the building have heard footsteps, "shuffling" noises, muffled voices, and what sounds like objects being dropped. Local residents have heard screams coming from the building in the middle of the night and seen lights turn on in the abandoned rooms. Many also have seen the shadows of human figures appearing in the building's smashed windows.

One visitor and her husband entered the building and then separated to take individual tours. He stayed in the basement near the entrance while she went upstairs to explore the second level. She was taking pictures of the remains of the Hospital's contents: rusty old beds and debris. When she walked to the middle of the second floor to take a picture of the hallway, she began to feel very agitated.

She took a deep breath and positioned the camera. As she took the picture she felt a huge gush of "charged" air...almost as if someone had run as fast as they could up to her face. At the same time she heard her husband yelling for her to come downstairs. He had been standing at the bottom of the stairs waiting for her when he saw a black shadow walking between the rooms of the former morgue. It blocked the light from a window about seven feet from the floor.

"I was waiting at the bottom of the stairs for my wife to return. As I stood there I was looking down the dark hallway, which

The basement of Sunland Hospital housed the facility's morgue. Until its demolition in 2006, it was littered with the rusty hospital beds once used for the hospital's mentally ill patients. A man exploring the building took this picture. Moments later he watched as a black shadowy mass blocked the light from the window at the end of the hall as it moved past.

ended with a large door with a single pane of glass at the top," said the husband.

"The atmosphere in the room became very heavy and then I *saw* it — a shadowy figure passed in front of the glass on the other side of the door, pausing slightly in the middle of the window. It wasn't like a shadow cast by someone...it seemed as if it was a person made of shadows.

"I called up the stairs to my wife and she didn't answer. I then began yelling for her. She peered down from the stairwell looking a little dazed. I thought maybe she had seen the same thing, or maybe something more eerie. Either way I was ready to go; and I said just that, 'It's time to go.'"

Local paranormal investigating groups have captured electronic voice phenomenon (EVP) in the building. EVPs are voices and sounds that are digitally recorded and generally not audible at the time of the recording.

EVPs captured in the Sunland Hospital building include voices saying:

"Don't go. Stay here."

"Watch your step, please."

A young sounding male voice saying "I'm David," and a faint voice whispering, "He's in the back ward crying."

Private Residence

There is a quiet, unassuming house in Tallahassee that residents and neighbors say not only is home to its current owners and residents, but its former owner who was known to most as Mr. Fern. Mr. Fern passed away from a heart attack in the back hallway of the home that leads to its three bedrooms.

Former residents believe Mr. Fern or something else wanders the hall and bedrooms. The doorknob of the front bedroom often turns by itself and is rattled back and forth. The closet door of that same bedroom is regularly opened and closed by unseen hands. Although the activity in the home occurs during both the day and night, former residents say the nighttime is especially noisy.

"I never felt unwelcome in the house, but I always walked through the hallway really quickly," says one former resident.

Guests who stay in the front bedroom often complain about scratching noises under the bed. On several occasions the homeowners' grandson stayed in the room by himself. He complained several times that there was scratching under the bed and a "noisy moose" in the corner. His mother lied down in his bed with him to calm him down, but after she also heard the noises, decided they should sleep in another room.

Former residents say that living in the home often was a lesson in patience. Items they used daily including shoes and favorite jewelry pieces often disappeared from where they were left. They would remain missing for days and then appear where they had been left or be put away if they had been left out.

One of the home's former residents had a favorite pair of earrings that she wore almost every day. On several occasions, they disappeared from her jewelry box and from the top of her dresser. They would be missing for days or even weeks. Then one day they would reappear in her jewelry box. Shoes left out in the living room or hallways were often found neatly placed in their respective closets.

The family's pets seemed to be aware of the uniqueness of the home as well. Residents say the family dog and cat often perked up and stared intently at something no one else in the house could see. The dog regularly barked and chased an unseen intruder down the hallway, and the cat seemed to be stalking something unseen throughout the house too.

The kitchen is a common area of unexplained activity in the home. One night residents were awakened by the sounds of someone walking around the kitchen fixing a drink. They walked out of their rooms and stared at each other in disbelief.

"We heard footsteps on the kitchen floor. Then we heard a cabinet open and close and ice clinking in a glass," says a former resident.

"It was so dark. There were no lights on. We didn't go in."

The family also learned not to argue too much in the home. On one Thanksgiving Day the home's residents and other family members were gathered in the kitchen talking and bickering. Suddenly, they watched as a pan that had been placed on the countertop lifted up and launched across the room slamming into the wall.

During another family dinner, a Thanksgiving serving platter that the family often joked was ugly and should be "accidentally" broken was lifted by unseen hands from a tightly packed shelf and thrown to the kitchen floor.

"We were all pretty quiet after that," said a former resident who was in the kitchen that day. "We didn't feel threatened in the house, as much as we felt something wanted us to know it was there."

(Author's note: Some names in the story have been changed to protect the identities of the contributors.)

Other Ghostly Locations...

The Quincy Leaf Theatre

"Doors slam. You hear objects hit the floor and footsteps walking all over the building. I used to get up and look around. I'm used to it now."

-- Bill Mock,
Theatre Managing Director

The Quincy Leaf Theatre was built in downtown Quincy, Florida in the 1940s. It was named after the golden tobacco leaf that was the staple crop of the area's economy. In the 1950s and 1960s the Leaf was considered the area's premier movie theatre.[20]

In the 1960s, single-screen theatres gave way to multiplex cinemas, and in 1980, the Leaf closed its doors. For years, it sat neglected and deteriorating.[20]

In 1983, the Quincy Music Group, an enthusiastic theatre group in need of a permanent home, began performing in churches and schools. That same year, the group purchased the Leaf Theatre and began renovations that not only gave new life to the once neglected building, but also shed light on some odd occurrences in the building. The group completed restoration of the theatre and, in the early 1980s, began offering locals and area visitors theatre productions including "Lil' Abner" and "Fiddler on the Roof." Longtime employee Bill Mock now manages the Theatre. When the renovations were complete and the group began rehearsing in the Theatre, strange things began happening.

Doors in the Leaf Theatre often are slammed shut by unseen hands. Staff hear objects moving and dropping to the floor of the auditorium and the storage and projection rooms. Footsteps are heard throughout the building when staff members know there is no one else in the Theatre.

"I have gotten to where I just ignore it now," says Bill, "but when I first started I would get up and inspect noises to find no one here and nothing having fallen. Doors that I heard slam shut were sitting wide open.

"There is so much unexplained noise in the auditorium," adds Bill.

During auditions for a production of "Plaza Street," one of the actors saw "figures" in the balcony area of the auditorium, including that of a man that she described as wearing khaki pants and a brown derby-style hat. She also saw a young girl wearing a dress and a young boy sitting in the third row of the auditorium.

Although there are many areas in the building where staff and visitors have experienced unexplained feelings and sightings, the auditorium seems to be the most active room. Over the years, many have seen these same apparitions in the auditorium. A housekeeper who worked at the Leaf Theatre for years often saw the apparition of a man wearing a brown belt and brown derby-style hat. When she was cleaning the auditorium, she would see him sitting in the third seat from the left. Bill says that particular seat will not stay closed.

The Quincy Leaf Theatre was the area's premiere movie theatre in its day. Now it showcases local drama talent and, staff say, some characters from the past.

"Every night after a show I go through and clean up and close up all of the seats," says Bill. "It never fails...moments later that seat is unfolded."

Town residents who remember the Leaf when it was a movie theatre say that staff often sat in that seat before and during the films to keep children from getting rowdy and running in the aisles.

One staff member felt a heavy presence pass through her at the top of the stairs that leads behind the auditorium into the former projection room.

One evening Bill was working in the auditorium at 3 a.m. repairing the stage. He set his drill down by his side. When he reached for it a moment later, it was gone. He got up and looked around. He found it four feet away from where he had left it.

"I continued to work so I could get it done," says Bill, "but the whole time I felt like someone was watching me."

At 4 a.m., Bill decided it would be better to try to get some sleep in the Theatre rather than drive home. He went into the lobby and lay down on the couch. But after several minutes, the feeling of being watched became so strong that he got up and turned on the lights and checked all of the rooms. When he was satisfied that he was alone, he turned off the lights and lay back down. Suddenly, the room became very cold. The feeling that something was there became so strong that he got up and went home.

"I tried to sleep. I was so tired," says Bill. "I couldn't shake the feeling that something was watching me and that that something really wanted me to leave."

Michael, a former manager, also experienced a sighting in the Theatre. He was working in the auditorium at 3 a.m. standing on the top of a ladder adjusting the lights for the next day's production. He glanced down toward the auditorium seats and saw a young girl in a dress standing in the third row watching him work. He immediately began stepping down the ladder. He asked her what she was doing in the theatre. When he got to the floor, she was gone.

"Michael was very upset about that," says Bill. "He looked for that little girl for an hour. He thought she was locked in the building."

One evening, an actor was rehearsing on stage when she looked out into the auditorium and saw the apparition of a thin, older woman with her hair up in a bun sitting in the back row next to the lobby door. She was wearing 1950s-style clothing.

Staff and performers often see something large moving in the darkness of a hole in the ceiling above the stairs that lead to the former projection room.

Quincy residents who had frequented the Theatre in the 1950s and 1960s confirmed that for years an older woman who dressed very conservatively worked at the concession stand. She would often sit in the last row of the auditorium by the lobby door so she could get up and return to her post when the movie ended.

Another area of the Theatre that Bill describes as "just a strange place" is the landing at the top of the stairs that leads behind the auditorium into the former projection room. The area is consistently twenty degrees colder than the rest of the building.

"...it makes the hair on the back of my neck stand up every time," says Bill.

It was in this exact area that the current housekeeper had an experience she will never forget. She was vacuuming the landing at the top of the stairs when she began to feel like she was "not alone." Suddenly, she felt a strong energy in the room and then felt something "pass through" her. She threw the vacuum down the stairs and hastily ran out of the Theatre.

Betty Davis, a local sensitive and the executive director of the ghost investigation group, The Big Bend Ghost Trackers, also had an experience in that area.

Betty saw a man wearing khaki colored pants and a brown belt standing at the top of the stairs. The man was frantically tapping his watch and gesturing with his arms for her to leave. Betty asked the man who he was and what he wanted. He continued to move about and tap his watch and gesture, but he did not respond to her.

Staff later discovered that the Theater's former projectionist often wore a brown belt and brown derby hat. Along with running the projection machine, his other responsibilities included clearing people from the auditorium so he could prepare for the next show.

Staff and actors often see movement in a hole in the ceiling above the second set of stairs that lead to the former projection room.

"You will be walking down the stairs and see something very large move over the opening of the hole," says Bill. Staff have climbed up and peeked in the hole that leads to the attic many times, but no one has been able to find any evidence of animals in the attic.

"I have been here for 25 years," said Bill. "You just never feel like you're alone here."

(Author's note: Some names in the story have been changed to protect the identities of the contributors.)

McLauchlin House of Havana

> *"One day an older gentleman came into the shop with his wife. He became very quiet and said, 'You are not alone here. There are several of them and they know you are here.'"*
>
> **-- Vicki Tonda,
> former McLauchlin shopkeeper**

The McLauchlin House of Havana was built in the 1840s. It was moved from a small town in Georgia to Havana in the 1990s, where it offers shopping excursions to local tourists and possibly a run-in with its former residents.

The McLauchlin House of Havana is nestled on a downtown corner in a collection of quaint shops and eateries located in the town of Havana, a popular weekend destination for those seeking to spend a relaxing Saturday shopping for antiques and collectables. The large farmhouse with its quintessentially southern rocking-chair front porch has not always been a landmark of downtown Havana.

The home was built in the 1840s in Decatur County, Georgia. It was the childhood home of Nellie McLauchlin Canton, who was born in the home in 1899 and later married her husband, Joe, in the very same home in 1919.[21]

Nellie remained in the home for much of her life, moving to Havana in her later years to be close to family. Nellie sold the McLauchlin House to local investors for one dollar with the promise that they would move it to Havana so she could be close to it.[21]

The home was relocated to Havana and has since served as a retail rental space for various shops. Over the years, the McLauchlin House has housed many different antique and specialty shops. Former shopkeepers' believe that Nellie was not the only one who wanted to stay close to her beloved McLauchlin House.

Shopkeepers and visitors often comment that they feel cold spots that are so pronounced they make their hair stand up on end. Merchandise is regularly moved from where it has been arranged and items are relocated from one end of the home to another.

Wendy Ebbers and Vicki Tonda, former McLauchlin shopkeepers, say there was a lot of activity in the home during Easter. To celebrate the holiday, shopkeepers displayed many different types of bunnies throughout the home: plush, plastic toys, and ceramic. They soon noticed that when they came into the house in the morning that the bunnies were not where they had left them.

"We would straighten the merchandise at the end of the day. When we came in the morning, there were bunnies everywhere," Wendy says. "It was as if someone had been playing with them.

"We thought it was our imaginations," adds Wendy, "but then we started finding bunnies on the bed, wrapped up in towels as if someone had tucked them in for the night."

One evening shopkeepers were promoting Breast Cancer Awareness Week. As part of the recognition, they were offering shop visitors a bench-painting demonstration. They had painted half of the bench that day and decided to leave it in the large hallway that runs from the front of the house through to the back rooms. They completed the evening's work, set the alarm, locked the doors, and went home for the night. When they arrived the next morning, there was a plush bunny sitting in the middle of the dry bench.

On another occasion, shopkeepers sold a large cabinet. As the customer waited, Wendy began removing all of the items that had been on display in the cabinet. As she cleared some decorative greenery from the top, she noticed that there were several bunnies tucked beneath it. She collected the bunnies and placed them off to the side. Both Wendy and the customer felt the atmosphere of the room suddenly change.

"The hallway became very cold," says Wendy.

One day an older gentleman and his wife came into the shop. He and his wife looked around quietly. The man approached Wendy and Vicki. He said, "You are not alone here. There are several of them. There is a little girl named Emily here. She died young. She is mischievous."

The man said the little girl appeared to be from the 1880s. She was eight or nine years old with brown hair that she wore in Victorian-style ringlets.

He said, "They know you are here."

When the man walked away, his wife explained that he was very "sensitive." She also said that she was very surprised that he had said anything about what he had seen because he usually keeps what he sees to himself.

Shopkeepers say there is a lot of activity in the back rooms of the home that are not accessible to the public. The rooms serve as storage and break areas, but at one time they were the living quarters for a McLauchlin family member. The man never married and spent most of his life in the back rooms of the home. He died there as well. A heavy smell of cigar and pipe smoke hangs in air of the rooms.

"It just happened one day," says Vicki. "I came in and one of the staff had five cans of air freshener on the counter. I went into the back room and it smelled very strongly of a pipe.

"From that day on, it was a regular occurrence. Some days the smell of smoke was so heavy, you couldn't stand being back there.

"It was not quiet in the back rooms," says Wendy. "You would be working up front and hear footsteps and movement. You'd swear there was someone back there.

"If I had to work late at night, I would turn up the radio, so I couldn't hear it."

One morning shopkeepers came in to find that the tables and chairs in the back room had been moved. Dishes had been taken from a buffet and a dinner place had been set at the table. The chair was pushed away from the table as if someone had been sitting there.

On another occasion, Vicki and her husband returned from an antique auction at about 10:30 p.m. By midnight, they had finished loading all of the new items into the shop. As they were leaving, Vicki remembered that she had forgotten to set the air conditioner. She went back into the home alone and walked down the long hallway toward the back room. She heard what she describes as a man's footsteps creaking loudly on the wood floor behind her. She called out to her husband, but he was still in the car.

Shopkeepers are not the only ones who have had a run in with the permanent resident of the back rooms of the McLauchlin

House. During the 2004 presidential election, a group of John Kerry supporters rented the back rooms as their headquarters.

One evening, a volunteer was alone in the home setting up chairs for a speaker who was to arrive the next day. She set a line of chairs for attendees. As she was walking down the hallway toward the front of the home, she heard the sound of chairs being dragged against the wood floors. She went back to investigate the noise—there was no one in the room, but several of the chairs had been turned around and were facing the opposite direction.

"I just smiled when she told me that," says Wendy. "No one believes until it happens to them.

"They are in that house. They didn't bother us. We just co-existed."

Private Residence in Port St. Joe

"I was in bed one night. All of the lights were out. I was looking for my Silky Terrier, Buckie. I heard him jump off of the bed. I got down on my hands and knees to look under the bed and I called, 'Buckie.' When I looked under the bed, there was something looking back at me."

-- Amy Ouellette,
homeowner

n 1992 Don Ouellette was looking to purchase a home in Port St. Joe when he discovered the former Lilus family home. The home had been on the market for years. The property was overgrown and the house in some disrepair. It was full of the furniture and belongings of its previous owners. Don purchased the home and held an estate sale, selling almost all of its contents. But...*when he moved into the home, he realized almost immediately that there was something strange about it.*

The Lilus family built the home in 1942. They owned a jewelry store in the small coastal town. They were well-known in the community, but seemed plagued by disaster. They had a daughter, Annalysa, and a son, Henry. Mrs. Lilus never saw her children grow up. She died of cancer in the home shortly after it was built. Annalysa was killed in a plane crash in her early 20s, and Henry contracted HIV in his 20s and by his 30s was suffering from AIDS.

In the early 1980s, there was not a lot of AIDS awareness. Shop owners often refused to help Henry and restaurants would not serve him. The one restaurant in town that would serve him was forced to deliver food to his home because customers threatened to leave if he was eating there. Henry died in his early 40s.

The home of Amy and Don Oullette of Port St. Joe as it looked when Don purchased it in 1992 and then after renovations. The Oullettes have heard disembodied voices in their living room. They have also seen the apparition of a small child on the second floor of the home and are aware of the constant presence of a set of eyes beneath their bed that wink and blink.

Mr. Lilus or "Big Henry," as he was known in town, lived alone in the house for several years until his own death. The distant relative of the Lilus's, who sold Don the home, died shortly after the sale.

The Ouellettes hear footsteps and furniture moving on the second floor of the home when they know no one is upstairs. Muffled voices are heard throughout the home. They have seen the apparition of a small child on the second floor and are aware of the constant presence of a set of eyes beneath their bed that wink and blink.

"Right away weird things started to happen," says Don. "Sometimes you hear voices and you go looking for a television that might be on, but they are all off."

When Don first moved into the home and had yet to remove all of the previous owners' belongings, he was sleeping downstairs in the living room by the fireplace. He awakened and saw a snake-like reptile that appeared to weigh about ten pounds flying slowly over his head. Don has since seen the reptile several more times in the living room and upstairs in the bedroom always flying slowly over his head when he is waking.

One evening, Don was in bed when he was awakened by what sounded like a child running wildly up the stairs and down the hallway. He sat up in bed and reached for his gun. A young boy appeared in the doorway of his bedroom and then ran to his bed and hopped up on the bed. The boy jumped on the bed three times and then hopped down and ran to the hallway. Don got up and ran down the hallway after it, but the noises stopped and he could not find the boy or anyone else in the home or outside.

The first night that Don's wife, Amy, stayed in the home she quickly became aware of its uniqueness. They were eating dinner in the dining room and Don was telling her about the history of the house and about Henry. As they were talking, the candles that were sitting on the table unlit bent toward Amy — they stayed that way all evening. In the morning they were straight again.

The Ouellettes often hear unexplained noises coming from upstairs—the sounds of a vacuum cleaner and furniture being moved around as if someone is cleaning. Locals say that Henry was a habitual cleaner.

"We hear big thuds upstairs," says Amy. "It's pretty common to be sitting downstairs and just hear someone running upstairs and thuds as if things are being dropped on the floor."

One night Amy's mother, Fay, was visiting. The family was sitting on the patio. She noticed that the blinds were moving and jokingly waved in their direction, saying, "Hello." The blinds started to move faster and continued moving for several minutes. That night Fay heard knocking on the front door. She ran down the stairs several times, but there was no one there.

"It seems to react to my mother," says Amy.

On another occasion, Amy had gone to sleep. Her mother and Don were downstairs in the living room. They heard a loud thud as if someone had fallen out of bed. They rushed up the stairs to check on Amy, who was asleep in bed.

One night Amy was home by herself. Don was at a restaurant with friends. Amy heard him come in the back door, open the refrigerator, and walk up the stairs. For several minutes, she sat and waited for him to come into the room or to say something.

"The stairs are wooden and they thunder when someone comes up or down," says Amy. "I could hear somebody upstairs."

Amy called Don on his cell phone to ask him what he was doing. He was still at the restaurant. Amy crept into the office and got the family gun. She sat in the living room. When Don returned, he checked the house. There was no one upstairs.

By far, the strangest occurrence in the Ouellette home are the eyes that appear nightly under the couple's bed. Amy was in bed one night. All of the lights were out. The couples' Silky Terrier, Buckie, jumped off of the bed. Amy got down to look for him. She bent down on her hands and knees to look under the bed. She didn't see Buckie...*but there was something looking back at her look.*

"Don made fun of me and then the next night when he looked under the bed," says Amy, "he jumped."

The eyes are green and cat-like in appearance. The Ouellettes have tried to poke them with a broom, but the broom goes straight through. They have blocked out all of the light with sheets to see if it is a reflection. But even with no light, the eyes are there blinking and winking. When the lights are turned on, they disappear.

"The little eyes look friendly," says Amy. "We show them to people all the time. They are there every night. Buckie slides under the bed and cuddles up next to them for several hours during the night."

On a recent vacation, Amy visited a psychic who described their home and their bedroom perfectly and told them that there was a spirit in their bedroom and that it loved their little dog. The Ouellettes often find wet footprints all around their home. They find them in the kitchen, the guest bedroom, the office, and even in the driveway.

"The activity seems to pick up whenever we make a change to the house, even if it's just decorations," says Amy.

The couple recently had their driveway paved. When it was completed, they discovered wet footprints on the concrete outside of their dining room window and just below the room that was once Annalysa's.

"They looked like little girl footprints," says Amy, "like someone had stepped in the wet grass with bare feet and then walked across the driveway. But they stayed there in that exact spot for a week."

On another occasion, Don had decided to paint over the pea-green colored walls in the room that was Annalysa's bedroom. He stayed up late painting the room. When he finished, he opened the windows and closed the bedroom door. When he woke in the morning and opened the door, the room was full of flies. The paint had been peeled off the walls in sheets and was piled in dry strips on the floor.

Shortly after the Ouellettes had hung Haitian artwork in the downstairs dining room, the activity picked up again. There were wet footprints throughout the home and the sounds of walking and furniture moving on the second floor.

On another occasion, the Ouellettes hired a house sitter to watch the home while they went on a cruise. When they returned, they found out that he had invited people to stay with him because after experiencing the house for one night, he was too frightened to stay overnight alone.

"When we got home, there were a lot of wet spots," says Amy.

One evening the Ouellettes were visiting with friends in their living room. They were sitting on the couch when they all heard the door to the downstairs bathroom open and close. The door is always kept shut to keep the dogs out.

They jumped up and walked down the hall to the door. The door was standing wide open. Also that week, Don's cigarette lighter disappeared. The couple had been looking for it for days. One night Amy was sitting in the office next to the living room. The lighter suddenly flew across the room and slid down the hallway toward Don as if someone had forcefully thrown it.

"We hear things all the time. When I'm here by myself, I talk to it and tell it not to scare me," says Amy.

"Overall, it's really not that bad. You get used to it. It's kind of nice."

Private Residence in Milton

"There is something out there."
-- Rai Orszak,
resident

rofessional performers Michael Wright and Rai Orszak were looking for a rural piece of land where they could retire, enjoy the quiet country, and let their dogs run loose. In 1992, the contract for the couple's Las Vegas show had come to an end. They were reunited with the Shrine Circus, where they had performed for years before moving to Las Vegas. They spent a lot of time traveling through Florida, and while passing through Milton, the couple discovered what they were looking for.

"The land just kept catching my eye," says Michael. "I felt drawn to it, but it wasn't for sale."

One day they drove by and there was a sale sign on the property. They made an offer and purchased the property that day.

For the first several years they owned the property, Michael and Rai were traveling so much with the Circus that they were only in the home for days or weeks at a time. When they decided to retire and move into the small house on the land, they began noticing strange things about the property and the home.

At night, when the rural property and the surrounding area was pitch black, they would hear knocking on the walls of the home and on the front door. But there was no one at the door or on the land.

"At first we thought someone was at the door," says Michael. "We would get up and open the front door. The dogs would run out into complete blackness. Now, we don't answer it."

The knocking progressed to banging. They began hearing voices and moaning coming from the walls. Unexplained sweet smells wafted through the rooms and down the hallway.

"The smells go right by you," says Michael. "Sometimes we follow it down the hallway. Then all of a sudden it's gone."

The couple found out later that others who had lived on the property had similar experiences. Based on their research the property, Michael and Rai believe the property was a slave cemetery in the 1800s. According to town records, the Nichol's family plantation was nearby. The land may also have been a location for mass burials during the Yellow Fever epidemic that swept through Florida in the 1800s. Two bodies have been exhumed near the land.

"The woman who sold us the property knew something was here," says Michael. "She told us that she was afraid we wouldn't buy the property if we knew."

Shortly after the two moved into the home permanently, Rai had gone out into the yard to help one of the couple's older dogs find its way back to the home. It was a hot summer night. He bent down to pick up the dog and was engulfed by heavy, cold air. Rai made his way back into the home with the dog and Michael went out to investigate.

"Rai came running into the house and said there is something out there," said Michael.

Michael took a picture of the ground where the cold spot was and when it was developed the letters KKK seemed to be carved into the ground. Michael started taking pictures of the yard nightly. The photos capture white wisps of swirling fog and bright splashes of colors in strange designs. Some of the photos seem to capture human-like and demon-like images. Michael lovingly refers to them as "spirits on the land." The cold spots on the land are an on-going phenomenon. The temperatures can range from eighty-five degrees in one area to forty-five degrees just inches away.

"When I cut the grass, it will be so hot and then all of a sudden there is a freezing-cold spot," says Michael.

Objects in the home often disappear. Rai, who designs costumes for Las Vegas and circus performers, says pieces of patterns disappear often as well as scissors, pencils, and measuring tape. On one occasion, Rai was in his sewing room working on a costume for a client. He got up from his chair and

was walking into the other room leaving a piece of fabric on the floor next to his chair. Moments later when he returned, the fabric was gone and in its place was a child's antique, fourteen-carat-gold chain.

Several psychics who have visited the property have

Photos taken on the grounds of the home of Michael Wright and Rai Orszak on Nichols Creek road in Milton often include unexplained smoky wisps that take human-like forms and circles that seem to move around the trees. *Courtesy of Michael Wright, "Spirits on the Land."*

reported the presence of a young mixed-race girl who was murdered on the property with poisoned tea. One psychic told Rai that he should not go out on the property at night because there is a spirit of a former slave on the land who is very angry and wants to hurt him.

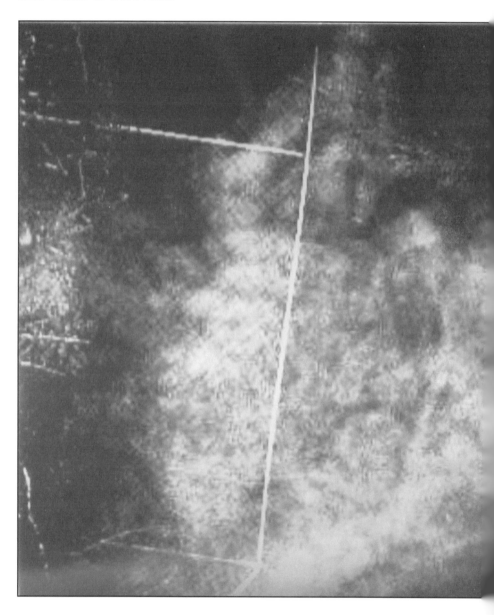

"I don't go out there," says Rai. "The farthest I go into the yard at night is to walk to the front gate. I pray all the way there and back and say out loud. 'I'll leave you alone, if you leave me alone.'"

Another psychic who visited the property collapsed in the yard from exhaustion and had to sit in the driveway for more

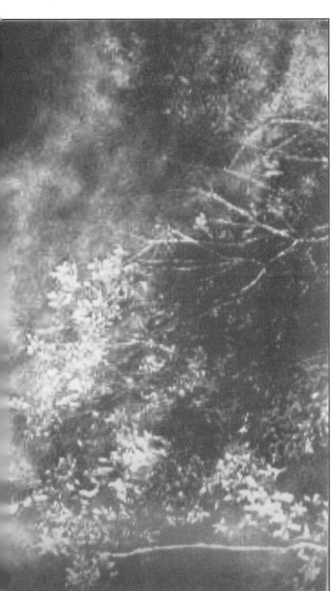

than an hour before she could return.

A woman who lives just across the street from the property came home from work one evening and saw a black man who seemed very out of place standing in her yard smiling at her garden. He was wearing old-fashioned looking bib overalls and a straw hat. The man tipped his hat to her and smiled. She reached down to pick up her bag from the car and when she looked back he was gone.

Later, Michael was digging in his yard and found the remains of a straw hat. Electronic devices in the home and on the property do not function properly. Flashlights will not stay lit on the grounds at night and cell phone and camera batteries drain in minutes.

"Anything electronic screws up in the house," says Michael. "I tell people to come with lots of extra batteries."

On one occasion, two teenage girls had visited the property to see if they could capture an image of something on their cell phone camera. The phone had a full charge when they walked into the yard. Moments later when they tried to take a picture, the battery was completely dead and the phone would not turn on.

One evening, Michael was talking on the phone. He put the phone down and walked over to lower the television volume. When he returned to the phone, the volume had gone back up. On another occasion, he was watching television and flipping through the channels when the channels began flipping by so fast that he couldn't see them. He removed the batteries from the remote control and the channels continued to flip rapidly.

Recently the couple was sitting in their living room.

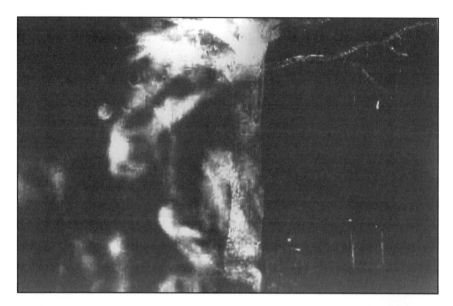

Rai heard a voice coming from the kitchen yelling, "Mike, Mike." Michael ran into the kitchen, but there was no one there.

"There is so much activity here. Sometimes I try to commune with them," says Michael. "And they do interact with me. I think we live on a portal or vortex. Sometimes, I ask them where they are buried."

Valdosta Southern Railroad Depot

> "It was 4, 4:30 a.m. It sounded like a woman's voice in a five-gallon bucket. She was saying, 'Is anybody home?'"
>
> -- Scott,
> current resident

The former Valdosta Southern Railroad Depot in Madison is now a private residence. Its current resident hears the disembodied voice of a woman booming through the home nightly.

In the early 1800s both passengers and freight traveled by steam engine train throughout the southern United States on the Florida and Georgia Railroad. Those who stopped in Madison arrived at the Valdosta Southern Railroad Depot.

The property is now owned by Apalachicola resident Betsy James, who inherited the Depot and its surrounding land from her father. The Depot is rented as a private residence. But those who stay in the home for any length of time realize quickly that they do not live alone. Current Depot resident, Scott, hears strange electrical noises as well as the disembodied voice of a woman booming through the home nightly.

Several neighbors who live on the quiet country road near the Depot have seen a man dressed in an old-fashion looking train conductor uniform walking down the road near the Depot and on its grounds.

Neighbors also regularly see an elderly woman, whom they know died years ago, peeking out of the Depot windows wearing her pink Sunday dress.

"I remember her," says Betsy. "My family used to drive her to church on Sundays. She was the last person to live in the Depot before Scott."

Scott is awakened every morning between 4 and 4:30 a.m. by a female voice that seems to be coming from the back bedroom booming loudly through the home. She says several sentences every time she speaks, but the words are not always discernable.

"Some nights the sound is so muffled it's difficult to understand what she is saying," says Scott. "Sometimes she asks, 'Is anyone home?'

"I don't answer her."

One night, as Scott was laying on the couch in the front room, her question came through loud and clear and was followed by a loud electrical snap that sounded as if was coming from the back bedroom.

"It sounded like a woman's voice talking in a five-gallon bucket asking the usual 'Is anybody home?'" says Scott. "The electrical snap was scary."

Strange electrical noises as well as a disembodied female voice boom from the back bedroom of the Valdosta Southern Railroad Depot in Madison.

During another early morning encounter, Scott was awakened at 4 a.m. by the door to the back bedroom continuously opening and slamming shut. He got up and inspected the door. The door was open and he could not find a reason for it to slam shut.

As he lay back down, the door began opening and slamming shut again. He got up to inspect the door three additional times that night. Each time, the door was open and he couldn't find a reason for it to slam shut.

"The slamming stopped when I got up and walked around," says Scott. "The second I lay down, it started again. Eventually, I just lay there and listened to it. It slammed every five minutes all night long."

On another occasion, Scott was working in the backyard just outside of the kitchen. He heard one of the kitchen chairs slide slowly across the floor. He walked into the kitchen to investigate, but nothing had been moved. He went back outside and continued his work. Fifteen minutes later he returned to the room. The kitchen chairs that had been sitting in different areas around the room were lined up at the dinner table.

"I didn't like that," says Scott.

Bibliography

1. The Gibson Inn of Apalachicola. "The Gibson Inn." www. gibsoninn.com/index.php.

2. Spohrer, Bill. "The House that Mr. Coombs Built." *The Coombs Inn of Apalachicola*.

3. NAS Pensacola. www.nappensacola.navy.mil/NASPensacola.

4. Garner, Tom M. "The Pensacola Lighthouse." Pensacola, Florida: Pensacola Historical Society, 1994.

5/6. Harms, Mrs. Alfred G. "Quarters A Ghost Stories." Pensacola, Florida: Dianne Levi/Pensacola Historical Society, United States Coast Guard.

7. Florida Center for International Technology, College of Education, University of South Florida; fcit.usf.edu/Florida.

8. The Pensacola Cultural Center. "Pensacola Little Theatre History." www.pensacolalittletheatre.com/aboutplt/historyplt. html.

9. Davis, Wendy. "Pensacola Historical Walking Tour." Pensacola, Florida: Pensacola Historical Museum.

10. Pensacola Victorian Bed & Breakfast of Pensacola. "The Pensacola Victorian Bed & Breakfast." www.pensacolavictorian. com/about.php.

11. Monticello Opera House of Monticello. "History of the Monticello Opera House." www.monticellofloridaoperahouse. com/page/page/4830762.htm.

12. McRory, Mary Oakley and Edith Clarke Barrows. "History of Jefferson County, Florida." Jefferson County, Florida: Kiwanis Club, 1935.

13. Jefferson County Cooperative Extension Service and the Jefferson County Planning Office. "Historic Monticello/Jefferson County." www.co.jefferson.fl.us/history/places.html.

14. City of Tallahasse, www.talgov.com/gov/facts/history.com

15. Goodwood Museum and Gardens. "Goodwood Museum and Gardens." www.goodwoodmuseum.org/history.html.

16. "Andrew Jackson: Good, Evil, & the Presidency"; www.pbs.org/kcent/andrewjackson/timeline.

17. Zimny, Michael. "The Knott House Museum." *Florida History and the Arts*. Tallahassee, Florida: 2003.

18. Florida Department of State. "The Knott House." www.flheritage.com/museum/sites/knotthouse/about.cfm.

19. Ensley, Gerald. "Demolition Closes Sunland Hospital's Chapter in History." Tallahassee, Florida: *Tallahassee Democrat*, November 5, 2006.

20. Quincy Music Theatre. "Detailed History of the Quincy Music Theatre by Season." www.qmtonline.com/histfull.htm.

21. Hunt, Bruce. "Visiting Small Town Florida." Sarasota, Florida: Pineapple Press, 2003.

Index